1. RESEARCH METHODS IN HISTORY

Historiography, Method, History Teaching

A Bibliography of Books and Articles in English,
1965-1973

by

ALEXANDER S. BIRKOS AND LEWIS A. TAMBS

LINNET BOOKS   1975

Library of Congress Cataloging in Publication Data

Birkos, Alexander S
  Historiography, method, history teaching.

  1. Historiography—Bibliography. 2. History—Study and
teaching—Bibliography. 3. History—Philosophy—Bibliography.
I. Tambs, Lewis A., 1927-joint author. II. Title.
Z6208.H5B57   016.907'2   74-19459
ISBN 0-208-01420-9

© 1975 by The Shoe String Press, Inc.
First published 1975 as a Linnet Book,
an imprint of The Shoe String Press, Inc.,
Hamden, Connecticut 06514

Printed in the United States of America

CONTENTS

Preface   ix

Part 1.   Research Methods in History [1:1 – 1:158]   1

Part 2.   Teaching of History   15
          A. College and University [2:A1 – 2:A93]   17
          B. Secondary School [2:B1 – 2:B132]   24

Part 3.   Historiography and Philosophy of History [3:1 – 3:526]   35

Part 4.   Historiographical Studies by Area   71
          Africa [4:1 – 4:9]   73
          Ancient and Classical [4:10 – 4:20]   73
          Asia [4:21 – 4:35]   74
          Australia [4:36]   75
          Austria [4:37]   75
          Brazil [4:38 – 4:41]   75
          Business History [4:42 – 4:44]   76
          Canada [4:45 – 4:46]   76
          Church History [4:47]   76
          Cultural History [4:48]   76
          Czechoslovakia [4:49 – 4:51]   77
          Eastern Europe [4:52]   77
          Economic History [4:53 – 4:57]   77
          Europe [4:58 – 4:71]   77
          France [4:72 – 4:84]   78
          Germany [4:85 – 4:101]   79
          Great Britain [4:102 – 4:122]   81
          Hungary [4:123 – 4:124]   82
          India [4:125 – 4:133]   83
          Italy [4:134 – 4:141]   83
          Labor History [4:142 – 4:144]   84
          Latin America [4:145 – 4:180]   84

Medical History [4:181 – 4:183]   87
Middle East [4:184 – 4:187]   87
Military History [4:188 – 4:194]   88
Netherlands [4:195 – 4:196]   88
Pacific Area [4:197 – 4:200]   89
Poland [4:201 – 4:204]   89
Scandinavia [4:205 – 4:207]   89
Science and Technology [4:208 – 4:209]   89
Spain [4:210 – 4:211]   90
United States [4:212 – 4:313]   90
USSR [4:314 – 4:337]   97
Yugoslavia [4:338 – 4:341]   99

Appendix: Checklist of Professional Periodical Literature   101
Historiography   103
Teaching of History   116

Author Index   119

PREFACE

English-speaking historians were confronted during the second half of the decade of the 1960's with a knowledge explosion and, especially in the United States, with a metaphysical crisis. The reverberations of these two phenomena have continued into the early 1970's.

This bibliography of books and articles in English, relating to historiography, method and history teaching published between 1965 and 1973 is designed not only to aid university, college and high school historians in their teaching, research and publication, but also to facilitate their awareness of new and often conflicting trends in current historiography. Future volumes covering works published since 1973 are being considered to keep this work up to date. It is thus designed to give continuing support to teachers and their students, who find themselves almost overwhelmed with the torrent of publications in their own specialty and who, consequently, have limited time to keep abreast of the broader trends in historiography and the philosophy of history.

The work is divided into four sections for convenient reference; 1: Research Methods in History, 2: Teaching of History, 3: Historiography and Philosophy of History, and 4: Historiographical Studies by Area. The entries in each section are arranged alphabetically by author or, in the cases where the Library of Congress so lists the work, by title. In addition to the author and title, the listing notes the edition—if it is other than the first—the place of publication, the publisher and the date of publication. Reprints of earlier works are included with the date of original issue in brackets [date].

Individual entries carry an introductory number (1:, 2:, 3: or 4:) indicating the section. This sectional number is followed by a numeral corresponding to the entry's alphabetical sequence within the section.

The Author Index is arranged alphabetically by name. The number or numbers after the author's name refer to the location in the compilation where his or her works will be found.

The compilers hope that this bibliography will enable its users to enlarge their historical knowledge and thus promote positive discussion on the teaching and researching of history and its various and changing philosophical interpretations.

Acknowledgments

The compilers would like to express their appreciation to Mr. Alvin Hughes, now Brother Stephen O.P., and Mr. Richard Super for their research efforts, and three members of the staff of Arizona State University, Ms. Vickie Jarvie of the Department of History and Ms. Katharine Phillips and Ms. Donna Wallock of the Center for Latin American Studies for their patience and skill in typing, proof reading, and indexing the manuscript.

The responsibility for any errors lies with the compilers alone.

A. S. B.
L. A. T.

1. RESEARCH METHODS IN HISTORY

1:1   Abrams, Philip, and David J. Rothman. "Sociology and History." *Past and Present,* vol. 52 (1971), pp. 118-134.

1:2   Adams, Richard N., ed. *Responsibilities of the Foreign Scholar to the Local Scholarly Community: Studies of U.S. Research in Guatemala, Chile and Paraguay.* Madison, Wis.: Latin American Studies Association, 1969.

1:3   ————. "Responsibilities of the Foreign Scholar to the Local Scholarly Community." *Current Anthropology,* vol. 12, no. 3 (1971), pp. 335-356.

1:4   Altick, Richard D. *The Scholar Adventurers.* New York: Free Press, 1966.

1:5   *Anglo-Romanian Conference on Mathematics in the Archaeological and Historical Sciences. Mamaia, Romania, 1970.* Hodson, R. F., D. G. Kendall and P. Tautu, eds. Edinburgh University Press, 1971.

1:6   Aydelotte, William O. "Quantification in History," *American Historical Review,* vol. 71, no. 3 (1966), pp. 803-825.

1:7   Baird, Robert D. "Interpretative Categories and the History of Religions," *History and Theory,* vol. 7, beiheft 8 (1968), pp. 17-30.

1:8   Barzun, Jacques. "History: The Muse and Her Doctors." *American Historical Review,* vol. 77, no. 1 (1972), pp. 36-64.

1:9   ————, and Henry F. Graff. *The Modern Researcher.* Revised edition. New York: Harcourt, Brace and World, 1970.

1:10 Beaumont, Roger A. "Images of War: Films as Documentary History," *Military Affairs,* vol. 35, no. 1 (1971), pp. 5-7.

1:11 Becker, Carl Lotus. *Detachment and the Writing of History: Essays and Letters of Carl L. Becker.* Edited by Phil L. Snyder. Westport, Conn.: Greenwood Press, 1972 [1958].

1:12 Beer, E. S. de. "A Reading of Gibbon," *Landfall,* vol. 19, no. 76 (1965), pp. 360-368.

1:13 Behavioral and Social Sciences Survey Committee. History Panel. *History as a Social Science.* David S. Landes and Charles Tilly. Englewood Cliffs, N.J.: Prentice-Hall, 1970.

3

4

1:14   Bender, Richard O. "Historical Criticism and the Bible," *Lutheran Quarterly,* vol. 17, no. 1 (1965), pp. 24-42.

1:15   Benson, Lee. *Toward the Scientific Study of History: Selected Essays of Lee Benson.* Philadelphia: Lippincott, 1972.

1:16   Berkhofer, Robert F. *A Behavioral Approach to Historical Analysis.* New York: Free Press, 1969.

1:17   Berkowitz, David Sandler. *Bibliographies for Historical Researchers.* Trial Edition. Waltham, Mass.: 1969.

1:18   Besancon, Alain. "Psychoanalysis: Auxiliary Science or Historical Method?" *Journal of Contemporary History,* vol. 3, no. 2 (1968), pp. 149-162.

1:19   Birkos, A. S. and Lewis A. Tambs. *Academic Writer's Guide to Periodicals, No. 1: Latin American Studies,* Kent, Ohio: Kent State University Press, 1971.

1:20   ———. *Academic Writers Guide to Periodicals, No. 2: East European and Slavic Studies.* Kent, Ohio: Kent State University Press, 1973.

1:21   Block, Jack. *Understanding Historical Research: A Search for Truth.* Glen Rock, N.J.: Research Publications, 1971.

1:22   Boni, Felix G. and Mitchell A. Selingsow. "Applying Quantitative Techniques to Quantitative History," *Latin American Research Review,* vol. 8, no. 2 (1973), pp. 105-110.

1:23   Boyer, Calvin J. *The Doctoral Dissertation as an Information Source: A Study of Scientific Information Flow.* Metuchen, N.J.: Scarecrow, 1973.

1:24   Braudy, Leo. *Narrative Form in History and Fiction.* Princeton, N.J.: Princeton University Press, 1970.

1:25   British Universities Film Council. *Films for Historians.* London: British Universities Film Council Ltd., 1972.

1:26   Brooks, Philip Coolidge. *Research in Archives: the Use of Unpublished Primary Sources.* Chicago: University of Chicago Press, 1969.

1:27   Burke, Collin B. "A Note on Self-Teaching, Reference Tools, and New Approaches in Quantitative History," *Historical Methods Newsletter,* vol. 4, no. 2 (1971), pp. 35-42.

1:28   Burnette Jr., O. Lawrence. *Beneath the Footnote: A Guide to the Use and Preservation of American Historical Sources.* Madison: State Historical Society of Wisconsin, 1969.

1:29   Butler, David. "Instant History," *New Zealand Journal of History,*
       vol. 2, no. 2 (1968), pp. 107-114.
1:30   Butterfield, L. H. "Editing American Historical Documents,"
       Proceedings of the Massachusetts Historical Society, vol. 78
       (1966), pp. 81-104.
1:31   Carney, T. F. "Content Analysis: A Review Essay," *Historical
       Methods Newsletter,* vol. 4, no. 2 (1971), pp. 52-61.
1:32   Child, Sargent Burrage, and Dorothy P. Holmes. *Check List of
       Historical Records Survey Publications: Bibliography of
       Research Project Reports.* Baltimore: Genealogical Publica-
       tions, 1969.
1:33   Clubb, Jerome M., and Howard Allen. "Computers and Historical
       Studies," *Journal of American History,* vol. 54, no. 3 (1967),
       pp. 599-607.
1:34   Cohen, Hennig. *The American Experience: Approaches to the
       Study of the United States.* Boston: Houghton Mifflin, 1968.
1:35   Crozier, Dorothy. "History and Anthropology," *International
       Social Science Journal,* vol. 17, no. 4 (1965), pp. 561-570.
1:36   Curtin, Philip D. "Field Techniques for Collecting and Processing
       Oral Data," *Journal of African History,* vol. 9, no. 3 (1968),
       pp. 367-395.
1:37   Curtis, L. P., Jr., ed. *The Historians Workshop: Original Essays
       by Sixteen Historians.* N. Y.: Alfred A. Knopf, 1970.
1:38   Davidson, J. W. "History, Art or Game? A Comment on 'The
       Purity of Historical Method,'" *New Zealand Journal of History,*
       vol. 5, no. 2 (1971), pp. 115-120.
1:39   Davisson, William I. *Information Processing: Applications in the
       Social and Behavioral Sciences.* New York: Appleton-Century-
       Crofts, 1970.
1:40   ———, and Marshall Smelser. "The Historian and the Computer,"
       Essex Institute Historical Collections, vol. 104, no. 2 (1968),
       pp. 109-126.
1:41   DePillis, Mario S. "Trends in American Social History and the Pos-
       sibilities of Behavioral Approaches," *Journal of Social History,*
       vol. 1, no. 1 (1967), pp. 37-60.
1:42   Diesing, Paul. *Patterns of Discovery in the Social Sciences: Observa-
       tions.* Chicago: Aldine-Atherton, 1971.
1:43   *The Dimensions of Quantitative Research in History.* Edited by

William O. Aydelotte, Allan G. Bogue and Robert William
Fogel. Princeton, N.J.: Princeton University Press, 1972.

1:44 Dollar, Charles M. "Innovations in Historical Research: A Computer Approach," *Computers and the Humanities,* vol. 3, no. 3 (1969), pp. 139-151.

1:45 ———, and Richard J. Jensen. *Historian's Guide to Statistics: Quantitative Analysis and Historical Research.* N.Y.: Holt, Rinehart and Winston, 1971.

1:46 Dowling, William C. "Avoiding the Warmed-Over Dissertation," *Scholarly Publishing,* vol. 4 (1973), pp. 235-238.

1:47 Dray, William, Richard G. Ely and Rolf Gruner. "Mandelbaum on Historical Narrative: A Discussion," *History and Theory,* vol. 8 (1969), pp. 275-294.

1:48 Elton, Geoffrey Rudolph. *Political History: Principles and Practice.* New York: Basic Books, 1970.

1:49 ———. *The Practice of History.* New York: Crowell, 1968.

1:50 Feinstein, Howard. "An Application of the Content of Identification for the Historian," *Journal of the History of Behavioral Science,* vol. 6, no. 2 (1970), pp. 147-150.

1:51 Finberg, H. P. R., ed. *Approaches to History: A Symposium.* Toronto: University of Toronto Press, 1969.

1:52 Finberg, H. R. P. and V. H. T. Skipp. *Local History: Objective and Pursuit.* Newton Abbott: David and Charles, 1967.

1:53 Finnegan, Ruth. "A Note on Oral Tradition and Historical Evidence," *History and Theory,* vol. 9, no. 2 (1970), pp. 195-201.

1:54 Fischer, David Hackett. *Historians' Fallacies: Toward a Logic of Historical Thought.* N.Y.: Harper & Row, 1970.

1:55 Fleming, John V. "Historians and the Evidence of Literature," *Journal of Interdisciplinary History,* vol. 4, no. 1 (1973), pp. 95-106.

1:56 Floud, Roderick. *An Introduction to Quantitative Methods for Historians.* Princeton, N.J.: Princeton University Press, 1973.

1:57 Formisano, Ronald P. "History and the Social Sciences: A Review Essay." *Historical Methods Newsletter,* vol. 4, no. 3 (1971), pp. 84-87.

1:58 Fuller, Daniel P. "The Resurrection of Jesus and the Historical Method," *Journal of Bible and Religion,* vol. 34 (1966), pp. 18-24.

1:59 Fyrth, Hubert J. and Maurice. *Science, History and Technology.*
London: Cassell & Company, 1969.

1:60 Gabel, Creighton and Norman R. Bennett, eds. *Reconstructing
African Culture History.* Boston: Boston University Press, 1967.

1:61 Galambos, Louis. "Business History and the Theory of the
Growth of the Firm." *Explorations in Entrepreneurial History,*
vol. 4, no. 1 (1966), pp. 3-16.

1:62 Gautam, Brijendra Pratap. *Researches in Political Science in India:
A Detailed Bibliography.* Foreword by A. V. Rao. Kanpur:
Oriental Publishing House, 1965.

1:63 Gemorah, Solomon. "Frederick J. Teggart: Scientific Historian of
the 'New History,'" *South Atlantic Quarterly,* vol. 68, no. 4
(1969), pp. 478-490.

1:64 Gentile, Giovanni. "Eighteenth-Century Historical Methodology:
De Soria's *Institutiones,*" *History and Theory,* vol. 4, no. 3
(1965), pp. 315-327.

1:65 Gilbert, Felix, comp. *Historical Studies Today.* Edited by Felix
Gilbert and Stephen R. Graubard. New York: W. W. Norton,
1972.

1:66 ———. "Intellectual History: Its Aims and Methods," *Daedalus,*
vol. 100, no. 1 (1971), pp. 80-97.

1:67 Goodman, Elizabeth J. "Citation Analysis as a Tool in Historical
Study: A Case Study Based on F. C. Donders and Mental Reac-
tion Times," *Journal of the History of Behavioral Science,* vol.
7, no. 2 (1971), pp. 187-191.

1:68 Gottschalk, Louis Reichenthal. *Understanding History: A Primer
of Historical Method.* 2nd edition. New York: Knopf, 1969.

1:69 Greenleaf, Richard E., comp. *Research in Mexican History:
Topics, Methodology, Sources and a Practical Guide to Field
Research.* Compiled and edited by Richard E. Greenleaf and
Michael C. Meyer for the Committee on Mexican Studies, Con-
ference on Latin American History. Lincoln: University of
Nebraska Press, 1973.

1:70 Gruner, R. "The Substantiation of Historical Statements,"
Durham University Journal, vol. 58, no. 2 (1966), pp. 75-85.

1:71 Hale, Richard W., Jr. "Methods of Research," *History News,*
vol. 24, no. 9 (1969), pp. 195-202.

1:72   Hancock, W. K. *Attempting History.* Canberra: Australian
        National University Press, 1969.
1:73   Hanham, H. J. "Clio's Weapons," *Daedalus,* vol. 100, no. 2 (1971),
        pp. 509-519.
1:74   Hartwell, R. M. "The Cause of the Industrial Revolution: An
        Essay on Methodology," *Economic History Review,* vol. 18,
        no. 1 (1965), pp. 164-182.
1:75   Hasslof, Olof. "Sources of Martime History and Methods of
        Research," *Mariner's Mirror,* vol. 52, no. 2 (1966), pp. 127-
        144.
1:76   Hearden, Harry. *Ideological Commitment and Historical Inter-
        pretation.* Cardiff: University of Wales Press, 1969.
1:77   Heller, Louis G. *Communicational Analysis and Methodology for
        Historians by L. G. Heller.* New York: New York University
        Press, 1972.
1:78   Henry, L. "The Verification of Data in Historical Demography,"
        Population Studies, vol. 22, no. 1 (1968), pp. 61-81.
1:79   Hermann, Charles F., and David J. Rothman. "An Attempt to
        Simulate the Outbreak of World War I," *American Political
        Science Review,* vol. 61, no. 2 (1967), pp. 400-416.
1:80   Higham, John. *Writing American History: Essays on Modern
        Scholarship.* Bloomington: Indiana University Press, 1970.
1:81   Hoenstine, Floyd G. *Guide to Genealogical and Historical
        Research in Pennsylvania,* 2nd edition, revised and enlarged,
        Holidaysburg, Pa.: 1966.
1:82   Hughes, H. Stuart. *History as Art and as Science: Twin Vistas on
        the Past.* N.Y.: Harper Torchbooks, 1965.
1:83   International Congress of Historical Sciences, *Vienna, 1965
        Rapports.* Hanns Leo Mikoletzky, ed. Horn Nieder-Oesterreich:
        Verlag F. Berger, 1966.
1:84   Jackson, Martin A. "Film As A Source Material: Some Prelim-
        inary Notes Toward a Methodology," *Journal of Interdiscipli-
        nary History,* vol. 4, no. 1 (1973), pp. 73-80.
1:85   Jacobs, Wilbur R. "Turner's Methodology: Multiple Working
        Hypotheses or Ruling Theory?" *Journal of American History,*
        vol. 54, no. 4 (1968), pp. 853-863.
1:86   Jones, Tom Bard. *Paths to the Ancient Past: Applications of the
        Historical Method to Ancient History.* New York: Free Press, 1967.

1:87 Katz, Michael B. "Quantification and the Scientific Study of
     History," *Historical Methods Newsletter,* vol. 6 (March 1973),
     pp. 63-68.
1:88 Kemnitz, Thomas M. "The Cartoon as a Historical Source,"
     Journal of Interdisciplinary History, vol. 4, no. 1 (1973), pp.
     81-94.
1:89 Kitson-Clark, George Sidney Roberts. *The Critical Historian.*
     New York: Basic Books, 1967, and London: Heinemann,
     1967.
1:90 ———. *Guide for Research Students Working on Historical
     Subjects.* 2nd edition, London: Cambridge University Press,
     1968.
1:91 Kuehl, Warren F. *Dissertations in History: An Index to Disserta-
     tions Completed in History Department of United States and
     Canadian Universities.* Lexington: University of Kentucky
     Press, 1965.
1:92 Leff, Gordon. *History and Social Theory.* University Ala.: Uni-
     versity of Alabama Press, 1969 and London: Merlin Press,
     1969.
1:93 Lipset, Seymour Martin, and Richard Hofstadter, eds. *Sociology
     and History.* New York: Basic Books, 1968.
1:94 Lorwin, Val R. "The Comparative Analysis of Historical Change:
     Nation-Building in the Western World," *International Social
     Science Journal,* vol. 17, no. 4 (1965), pp. 594-606.
1:95 ———, and Jacob M. Price, eds. *The Dimensions of the Past:
     Materials, Problems and Opportunities for Quantitative Work
     in History.* New Haven: Yale University Press, 1972.
1:96 McCalmon, George and Christian Moe. *Creating Historical Drama:
     A Guide for the Community and the Interested Individual.*
     Foreword by Louis C. Jones. Carbondale: Southern Illinois
     University Press, 1965.
1:97 Mallard, William. "Method and Perspective in Church History: A
     Reconsideration," *Journal of the American Academy of
     Religion,* vol. 36, no. 4 (1968), pp. 345-365.
1:98 Mandelbaum, Maurice H. *The Problem of Historical Knowledge:
     An Answer to Relativism.* New York: Harper & Row, 1967.
1:99 Marczewski, Jean. "Quantitative History," *Journal of Contempo-
     rary History,* vol. 3, no. 2 (1968), pp. 179-191.

1:100   Marsak, Leonard Mendes, ed. *The Nature of Historical Inquiry.*
        New York: Holt, Rinehart and Winston, 1970.
1:101   Mitchell, Roger. "Oral Tradition and Micronesian History: A
        Microcosmic Approach," *Journal of Pacific History,* vol. 5
        (1970), pp. 33-41.
1:102   Modern Language Association. *The MLA Style Sheet.* 2d edi-
        tion. New York: Modern Language Association, 1970.
1:103   Moraze, Charles. "The Application of the Social Sciences to
        History," *Journal of Contemporary History,* vol. 3, no. 2
        (1968), pp. 207-215.
1:104   Mozley, Ann. "Oral History," *Historical Studies. Australia and
        New Zealand,* vol. 12, no. 48 (1967), pp. 571-578.
1:105   Murphy, George G. S. "Historical Investigation and Automatic
        Data Processing Equipment," *Computers and the Humani-
        ties,* vol. 3, no. 1 (1968), pp. 1-13.
1:106. ———, and M. G. Mueller. "On Making Historical Techniques
        Specific: 'Real Types' Constructed with a Computer,"
        History and Theory, vol. 6, no. 1 (1967), pp. 14-32.
1:107   Nappen, Marc and Norman McNatt. "Microfilming for the
        Historian," *History Teacher,* vol. 5, no. 2 (1972), pp. 57-60.
1:108   Newman, Fred D. *Explanation by Description: An Essay on
        Historical Methodology.* Paris, The Hague: Mouton, 1968.
1:109   Noggle, Burl. "A Note on Historical Editing: The Wilson 'Papers'
        in Perspective," *Louisiana History,* vol. 8, no. 3 (1967), pp.
        281-297.
1:110   National Colloquium on Oral History, 1st, Lake Arrowhead,
        Calif., 1966. *Oral History at Arrowhead: Proceedings.* Edited
        by Elizabeth I. Dixon and James V. Mink. Los Angeles: Oral
        History Association, 1967.
1:111   Penner, Hans H. "Myth and Ritual," *History and Theory,* beiheft
        8 (1968), pp. 46-57.
1:112   Perkins, Whitney T. "Science in the Study of International
        Politics: Imperialism or Integration?" *Polity,* vol. 2, no. 3
        (1970), pp. 367-373.
1:113   Pflug, Gunther. "The Development of Hitorical Method in the
        Eighteenth Century," *History and Theory,* vol. 10, bei. 11
        (1971), pp. 1-23.
1:114   Phillips, Derek L. *Abandoning Method: Sociological Studies*

in Methodoloty. San Francisco: Jossey-Bass, 1973.

1:115 Pitt, David C. *Using Historical Sources in Anthropology and Sociology.* New York: Holt, Rinehard and Winston, 1972.

1:116 Pomper, Philip. "Problems of Naturalistic Psycho-History," *History and Theory,* vol. 12, no. 4 (1973), pp. 367-388.

1:117 Postan, Michael Moissey. *Fact and Relevance: Essays on Historical Method.* Cambridge: Cambridge University Press, 1971.

1:118 Poulton, Helen J. *The Historian's Handbook: A Descriptive Guide to Reference Works* by Helen J. Poulton with the assistance of Marguerite S. Howland. Foreword by Wilbur S. Shepperson, 1st ed., Norman: University of Oklahoma Press, 1972.

1:119 Price, Jacob M. "Recent Quantitative Work in History," *History and Theory,* beiheft 9 (1969), pp. 1-13.

1:120 Rashevsky, Nicolas. *Looking at History Through Mathematics.* Cambridge, Mass.: M.I.T. Press, 1968.

1:121 Rasila, Viljo. "The Use of Multivariable Analysis in Historical Studies," *Economy and History,* vol. 13 (1970), pp. 24-53.

1:122 Rowney, Don Karl. *Quantitative History: Selected Readings in the Quantitative Analysis of Historical Data.* Edited by Don Karl Rowney and James Q. Graham, Jr. Homewood, Ill.: Dorsey Press, 1969.

1:123 Rundell, Walter, Jr. *In Pursuit of American History: Research and Training in the United States.* Norman: University of Oklahoma Press, 1970.

1:124 Runes, Dagobert D. *Crosscuts Through History.* New York: Philosophical Library, distributed by Book Sales, 1965.

1:125 Ryding, Nils Erik. *The Concept "Cause" as Used in Historical Explanation.* Translated into English by Mary Wentz. Lund, Sweden: C. W. K. Gleerup, 1965.

1:126 Sakmann, Paul. "The Problem of Historical Method and of Philosophy of History in Voltaire," *History and Theory,* vol. 10, beiheft 11 (1971), pp. 24-59.

1:127 Schellenberg, T. R. *The Management of Archives.* New York: Columbia University Press, 1965.

1:128 Schofield, R. D. "Historical Demography: Some Possibilities and Some Limitations," *Transactions of the Royal Historical Society,* vol. 21 (1971), pp. 119-132.

1:129   Shafer, Robert Jones, ed. *A Guide to Historical Method.* Homewood, Ill.: Dorsey Press, 1969.
1:130   Silbey, Joel H. "Clio and Computers: Moving into Phase II, 1970-1972," *Computers and Humanities,* vol. 7 (November 1972), pp. 67-79.
1:131   Simon, Julian L. *Basic Research Methods in Social Science.* New York: Random House, 1968.
1:132   Skolnick, M. H. "A Computer Program for Linking Records." *Historical Methods Newsletter,* vol. 4, no. 4 (1971), pp. 114-125.
1:133   Small, Melvin, ed. *Public Opinion and Historians: Interdisciplinary Perspectives.* Detroit: Wayne State University Press, 1970.
1:134   Smith, Morton. "Historical Method in the Study of Religion," *History and Theory,* beiheft 8 (1968), pp. 8-16.
1:135   *Studies in Quantitative History and the Logic of the Social Sciences.* Middletown, Conn.: Wesleyan, University Press, 1969.
1:136   Symmons-Symonolewicz, Konstantin. "Nationalist Movements: An Attempt at a Comparative Typology," *Comparative Studies in Society and History,* vol. 7, no. 2 (1965), pp. 221-230.
1:137   Szreter, R. "History and the Sociological Perspective in Educational Studies," *University of Birmingham Historical Journal,* vol. 12, no. 1 (1969), pp. 1-19.
1:138   Taft, William Howard. *Newspapers as Tools for Historians.* Columbia, Mo.: Lucas Bros., 1970.
1:139   Tholfsen, Trygve R. *Historical Thinking: An Introduction.* New York: Harper & Row, 1967.
1:140   Thrupp, Sylvia L. "Comparative Studies in Society and History: A Working Alliance Among Specialists," *International Social Science Journal,* vol. 17, no. 4 (1965), pp. 644-654.
1:141   Tillot, P. M. "The Analysis of Census Returns." *Local Historian,* vol. 8, no. 1 (1968), pp. 2-10.
1:142   Tilly, Charles. "In Defense of Jargon," *Canadian Historical Association Annual Report* (1966), pp. 178-186.
1:143   ———. "The Historian as Editor: Francis Parkman's Reconstruction of Sources in Montcalm and Wolfe," *Journal of American History,* vol. 53, no. 3 (1966), pp. 471-486.
1:144   Topolski, Jerzy. "The Model Method in Economic History,"

Journal of European Economic History, vol. 1 (Winter 1972), pp. 713-726.

1:145   Tucker, K. A. "Business History: Some Proposals for Aims and Methodology," *Business History,* vol. 14, no. 1 (1972), pp. 1-16.

1:146   Turner, C. M. "Sociological Approaches to the History of Education," *British Journal of Education Studies,* vol. 17, no. 2 (1969), pp. 146-155.

1:147   Vann, Richard T. "History and Demography." *History and Theory,* beiheft 9 (1969), pp. 64-78.

1:148   Vansina, Jan. *Oral Tradition: A Study in Historical Methodology.* Translated by H. M. Wright. Chicago: Aldine Publishing Co., 1965 [1961].

1:149   Vincent, John Martin. *Aids to Historical Research.* Freeport, N.Y.: Books for Libraries Press, 1969.

1:150   Vitzthum, Richard C. "Henry Adams Paraphrase of Sources in the *History of the United States,*" *American Quarterly,* vol. 17, no. 1 (1965), pp. 81-91.

1:151   Vries, Leonard de. *Panorama 1842-1865; The World of the Early Victorians as Seen Through the Eyes of the Illustrated London News.* Foreword by Arthur Bryant, Introduction by W. H. Smith, text abridged by Ursula Robertshaw. London: Murray, 1967.

1:152   Ware, Caroline F., ed. *The Cultural Approach to History.* Port Washington, N.Y.: Kennikat Press, 1965 [1940].

1:153   Watson, Robert I. "Prescriptions as Operative in the History of Psychology," *Journal of the History of Behavioral Science,* vol. 7, no. 4 (1971), pp. 311-322.

1:154   White, Gerald T. "The Business Historian and His Sources," *American Archivist,* vol. 30, no. 1 (1967), pp. 19-31.

1:155   Whitehill, Walter Muir. "A Fable for Historical Editors," *New England Quarterly,* vol. 39, no. 4 (1966), pp. 513-515.

1:156   Winks, Robin, ed. *The Historian as Detective: Essays on Evidence.* 1st edition, New York: Harper & Row, 1969.

1:157   Wright, Monte D. "Demography for Historians," *Rocky Mountain Social Science Journal,* vol. 7, no. 2 (1970), pp. 1-10.

1:158   Young, Pauline. *Scientific Social Surveys and Research.* 4th edition. Englewood Cliffs, N.J.: Prentice-Hall, 1966.

2. TEACHING OF HISTORY

A. COLLEGE AND UNIVERSITY

2:A1   Adams, Herbert Baxter. *Methods of Historical Study.* New
        York: Johnson Reprint Corp., 1973 [1884].
2:A2   Bader, Thomas M. "A Second Field for Historians of Latin
        America," *Journal of Inter-American Studies and World
        Affairs,* vol. 12, no. 1 (1970), pp. 45-54.
2:A3   Ballard, Martin, ed. *New Movements in the Study and Teaching
        of History.* Bloomington: Indiana University Press, 1970,
        and London: Maurice Temple Smith, 1970.
2:A4   Barlow, George and Brian Harrison, eds. *History at the Uni-
        versities: A Comparative and Analytical Guide to History
        Syllabuses at Universities in the United Kingdom.* London:
        Historical Association, 1966.
2:A5   Billington, Monroe. "College Courses in Southern History: A
        Survey," *Journal of Southern History,* vol. 31, no. 3 (1965),
        pp. 305-317
2:A6   Blassingame, John W. "Black Studies: An Intellectual Crisis,"
        American Scholar, vol. 38, no. 4 (1969), pp. 548-561.
2:A7   Blows, Roger Philip, ed. *History at the Universities: A Compara-
        tive and Analytical Guide to Degree Courses in History in
        the United Kingdom.* 3d ed. London: Historical Association,
        1971.
2:A8   Bodin, Jean. *Method for the Easy Comprehension of History.*
        Translated by Beatrice Reynolds. New York: Octagon Books,
        1966.
2:A9   Brooke, Christopher N. L. "The Teaching of Diplomatic,"
        Journal of the Society of Archivists, vol. 4, no. 1 (1970),
        pp. 1-9.
2:A10   Buah, F. K. *A New History for Schools and Colleges.* London:
        Macmillan, 1967.
2:A11   Burston, W. H. and D. Thompson, eds. *Studies in the Nature
        and Teaching of History.* London: Routledge & K. Paul;

New York: Humanities, 1967; 2d rev. ed., London: Methuen, 1972.

2:A12   Buzanski, Peter M. "The Knowledge Explosion and the Teaching of American History: The Crowell American History Series," *Studies in History and Society,* vol. 1, no. 2 (1969), pp. 41-46.

2:A13   Cantor, Norman F. and Richard L. Schneider. *How to Study History.* New York, Crowell, 1967.

2:A14   Carpenter, Peter. *History Teaching, the Era Approach.* Cambridge: University Press, 1965.

2:A15   Cate, James Lea. *The 1965 History Institutes Revisited.* For the American Historical Association, 1966.

2:A16   Clegern, Wayne M. "Teaching Latin American History," *History Teacher,* vol. 5, no. 1 (1971), pp. 19-25.

2:A17   College Publishing Corporation. *How to Pass Graduate Record Examination; Advanced Test: History.* New York, 1967.

2:A18   ―――. *What Do You Know About History: Key Questions and Correct Answers.* New York, 1967.

2:A19   Commager, Henry Steele. *The Study of History.* Columbus, Ohio: C. E. Merrill Books, 1966.

2:A20   Daniels, Robert Vincent. *Studying History: How and Why.* Englewood Cliffs, N.J.: Prentice Hall, 1966, 2d ed., 1972.

2:A21   Davis, Gerald H. and David M. Laushey, "Tampering With the Temporal Order," *History Teacher,* vol. 5, no. 3 (1972), pp. 40-44.

2:A22   Davis, Ralph H. *Good History and Bad: An Inaugural Lecture Delivered in the University of Birmingham on 11th November.* Birmingham, Eng.: University of Birmingham, 1972.

2:A23   Donnitz, Myer. "Efforts of Eliminating Prejudice in Textbooks," *Patterns of Prejudice,* vol. 5, no. 3 (1971), pp. 7-10.

2:A24   Droysen, Johann Gustav. *Outline of the Principles of History. (Grundriss der Historik)* With a biographical sketch of the author by Hermann Kruger. Translated by E. Benjamin Andrews. New York: H. Fertig, 1967.

2:A25   Edwards, S. F. "The Columbus to Castro Course in Latin American Studies," *Journal of Inter-American Studies and World Affairs,* vol. 12, no. 4 (1970), pp. 602-611.

2:A26   Ekman, Ernst. "The Teaching of Scandinavian History in the

United States," *Scandinavian Studies,* vol. 37, no. 3 (1965), pp. 259-270.

2:A27 Elton, Geoffrey Rudolph. *The Future of the Past: An Inaugural Lecture.* London: Cambridge U. P., 1968.

2:A28 ————. "Second Thoughts on History at the Universities," *History,* vol. 54, no. 180 (1969), pp. 60-67.

2:A29 Emmett, Richard S. *Report on the "Caesar Unit": Some Linguistic Skills for History Students by David McNeill.* Cambridge, Mass.: Educational Services, 1965.

2:A30 Enteen, George M. "The History Faculty of Moscow State University," *Russian Review,* vol. 28, no. 1 (1969), pp. 66-76.

2:A31 Fines, John. *A Select Bibliography of the Teaching of History in the United Kingdom.* London: Historical Association, 1969.

2:A32 Gawronski, Donald V. *History: Meaning and Method.* Iowa City, Ia.: Sernoll, 1967, rev. ed., Glenview, Ill.: Scott, Foreman, 1969.

2:A33 Geddes, John A. *How to Study History.* New York: Vantage Press, 1965.

2:A34 Grannis, Joseph C. "The Social Studies Teacher and Research on Teacher Education," *Social Education,* vol. 34, no. 3 (1970), pp. 291-301, 315.

2:A35 Grivas, Theodore and Ted C. Hinckley. "Insights on a Pioneer NDEA Institute in American History," *California Social Science Review,* vol. 5, no. 3 (1966), pp. 15-20.

2:A36 Gruber, Edward C. *History: Advanced Tests for the Graduate Record Examination.* New York: Arco Publishing, 1964.

2:A37 *Handbook for History Teachers.* Green, C. W. and W. H. Burston, eds. London: Methuen, 1962. Second edition, 1970.

2:A38 Hanke, Lewis. "The Coming Revolution in the Teaching of Latin American History," *Social Education,* vol. 34, no. 6 (1970), pp. 608-612.

2:A39 Hansen, Lorentz I. *Invitation to the Romance of History.* New York: Exposition Press, 1961.

2:A40 Harper, Charles W., Jr. "Improving Preparation and Placement of American History Teachers," *Social Studies,* vol. 59, no. 6 (1968), pp. 269-271.

2:A41 Harrison, Brian. "History at the Universities 1968: A Commentary," *History*, vol. 53, no. 179 (1968), pp. 357-380.

2:A42 Herbst, Jurgen. "Theoretical Work in History in American University Curricula," *History and Theory*, vol. 7, no. 3 (1968), pp. 336-354.

2:A43 Hinckley, Theodore C., and J. W. Sutherland. "Teaching History via Instructional Television," *California Social Science Review*, vol. 5, no. 1 (1965), pp. 24-30.

2:A44 *Historical Study in the West: France, Great Britain, Western Germany, the United States*. Michel François and others. Introduction by Boyd C. Shafer. New York: Appleton-Century-Crofts, 1968.

2:A45 *History as Social Science*, edited by David S. Landes and Charles Tilley. Report of the History Panel of the Behavioral and Social Sciences Survey Committee. Englewood Cliffs, N.J.: Prentice-Hall, Inc., March, 1971.

2:A46 *History Today in USA, Britain, France, Italy, Germany, Poland, India, Czechoslovakia, Spain, Holland, Sweden*. Walter Laqueur, George L. Mosse, eds., Jane Degras, Ernest Hearst, assistant eds. London: Weidenfeld and Nicolson, 1967.

2:A47 Jones, Gareth E. "Towards a Theory of History Teaching," *History*, vol. 55, no. 183 (1970), pp. 54-64.

2:A48 Jones, Howard Mumford. "Uses of the Past in General Education," *Harvard Educational Review*, vol. 36, no. 1 (1966), pp. 3-16.

2:A49 Jones, Thomas M. "A Broader Cultural Span for Teaching Medieval History," *Liberal Education*, vol. 53, no. 2 (1967), pp. 233-243.

2:A50 Jones, Tom Bard. *Paths to the Ancient Past: Applications of the Historical Method to Ancient History*. New York: Free Press, 1967.

2:A51 Kent, Sherman. *Writing History*. Revised with the assistance of James T. Schleifer. 2nd edition. New York: Appleton-Century-Crofts, 1967.

2:A52 Kitagawa, Joseph M. "The Making of a Historian of Religions," *Journal of the American Academy of Religion*, vol. 36, no. 3 (1968), pp. 191-202.

2:A53 Kitson-Clark, George Sidney Roberts. *The Critical Historian*. New York: Basic Books, 1967.

2:A54   ———. *Guide to Research Facilities in History in the Universities of Great Britain and Ireland.* 2nd edition by G. Kitson-Clark and G. R. Elton. Cambridge, Eng.: University Press, 1965.

2:A55   Kochar, S. K. *The Teaching of History.* Delhi: Sterling Publishers, 1967.

2:A56   Koenig, Duane. "Teaching the Freshman Civilization Section," *Social Studies,* vol. 58, no. 4 (1967), pp. 159-161.

2:A57   Kuklick, Bruce. "History as a Way of Learning," *American Quarterly,* vol. 22 (1970), pp. 609-628.

2:A58   La Nauze, John Andrew. *Presentation of Historical Theses: Notes for University Students.* Melbourne: Melbourne University Press, 1966.

2:A59   Landes, David. "The Treatment of Population in History Textbooks," *Daedalus,* vol. 97, no. 2 (1968), pp. 363-384.

2:A60   Langer, William Leonard, ed. *An Encyclopedia of World History: Ancient, Medieval, and Modern.* 4th edition, revised and enlarged. Boston: Houghton Mifflin, 1968.

2:A61   Langlois, Charles Victor. *Introduction to the Study of History.* Translated by G. G. Berry, with Preface by F. York Powell. New York: Barnes & Noble, 1966, and London: Cass, 1966.

2:A62   Lucid, Robert F. "American Studies Programs in the United States: A Quantitative Survey," *American Quarterly,* vol. 18, no. 2 (1966), pp. 357-363.

2:A63   Mahon, John K. "Teaching and Research on Military History in the United States," *Historian,* vol. 27, no. 2 (1965), pp. 170-183.

2:A64   Meel, Edward J. "The Revolution in Audio-Visual Instruction: Has It Hit the Colleges?" *Studies in History and Society,* vol. 1, no. 1 (1968), pp. 12-17.

2:A65   Mörner, Magnus. "The Study of Latin American History Today," *Latin American Research Review,* vol. 8, no. 2 (1973), pp. 75-100.

2:A66   Nugent, Walter T. K. *Creative History: An Introduction to Historical Study.* Philadelphia: Lippincott, 1967, 2nd ed., 1973.

2:A67   Perman, Dagmar Horna, ed. *Bibliography and the Historian; the Conference at Belmont of the Joint Committee on*

        Bibliographical Service to History, May, 1967. Santa Barbara,
        Calif.: CLIO, 1968.

2:A68 Pierre, Bessie Louise. *Public Opinion and the Teaching of
        History in the United States.* New York: Da Capo Press,
        1970.

2:A69 *Oxford Lectures on History,* 1904-1923. Freeport, N.Y.: Books
        for Libraries Press, 1966.

2:A70 Price, Joedd. "The Teaching of History: A Few Remarks to
        Latin American Historians by a Graduate Student," *Secolas,*
        vol. 2, no. 1 (1971), pp. 27-38.

2:A71 Reid, Inez Smith. "An Analysis of Black Studies Programs,"
        Pan-African Journal, vol. 2, no. 3 (1969), pp. 284-298.

2:A72 Rundell, Walter, Jr. "Clio's Ways and Means: A Preliminary
        Report on the Survey [on the Use of Original Sources in
        Graduate History Training]," *The Historian,* vol. 30, no. 1
        (1967), pp. 20-40.

2:A73 ———. *In Pursuit of American History: Research and Training
        in the United States.* 1st edition. Foreword by James B.
        Rhoads. Norman: University of Oklahoma Press, 1970.

2:A74 ———. "Southern History from Local Sources: A Survey of
        Graduate History Training," *Journal of Southern History,*
        vol. 34, no. 2 (1968), pp. 215-226.

2:A75 Seminar on the Study of History and College Teaching. *The
        Study of History and College History Teaching; Report of
        the Seminar Held in Patiala, March 29-April 17, 1965.* John
        C. B. Webster, ed. Patiala: Punjabi University, 1965.

2:A76 Shera, Jesse Hauk. *Historians, Books and Libraries: A Survey
        of Historical Scholarship in Relation to Library Resources,
        Organization and Services.* New York: Greenwood Press,
        1969 [1953].

2:A77 Simms, L. Moody, Jr. "American Intellectual History," *Social
        Studies,* vol. 59, no. 6 (1968), pp. 248-250.

2:A78 Smith, Goldwin Albert, comp. *The Professor and the Public:
        The Role of the Scholar in the Modern World.* Detroit:
        Wayne State University Press, 1972.

2:A79 Spector, Robert M. "Psychology in the Training of the Profes-
        sional Historian," *Social Studies,* vol. 62, no. 5 (1971), pp.
        223-225.

2:A80   ———. "The Time-Factor and the Teaching of College History,"
           Social Studies, vol. 57, no. 4 (1966), pp. 164-169.
2:A81   Spencer, Thomas E. "On the Place of the Negro in American
           History," *Social Studies,* vol. 60, no. 4 (1969), pp. 150-158.
2:A82   Still, Bayrd. "The Teaching of American Urban History,"
           Journal of American History, vol. 55, no. 4 (1969), pp. 843-
           847.
2:A83   *Studies in History.* NDEA Institute Faculty. Wichita, Kan.:
           Wichita State University, 1969.
2:A84   *The Teaching of History.* Joseph S. Roucek, ed. New York:
           Philosophical Library, 1967.
2:A85   Thompson, James Westfall. *A History of Historical Writing.*
           Collaboration of Bernard J. Holm. Gloucester, Mass.: P.
           Smith, 1967 [1942].
2:A86   Van Jaarsveld, Floris Albertus and J. E. Rademeyer. *Theory
           and Method of Teaching History.* Johannesburg: Voortrek-
           kerpers, 1964.
2:A87   Ward, Paul L. *Elements of Historical Thinking.* Washington:
           American Historical Association, 1971.
2:A88   Warren, Donald, Jr. "The 'Atlantic Vocation' and Teaching
           Brazilian History," *Luso-Brazilian Review,* vol. 5, no. 1
           (1968), pp. 75-85.
2:A89   Warriner, Helen P. *The Effectiveness of the Use of Foreign
           Languages in Teaching Academic Subjects.* Richmond:
           Division of Educational Research, State Dept. of Education,
           1968.
2:A90   Wenden, D. J. "Films and the Teaching of Modern History,"
           History, vol. 55, no. 184 (1970), pp. 216-219.
2:A91   Winkler, Henry R. "History in the Study and in the Schools,"
           Ohio History, vol. 75, no. 2-3 (1966), pp. 166-177.
2:A92   Woodward, C. Vann. "Clio with Soul," *Journal of American
           History,* vol. 56, no. 1 (1969), pp. 5-20.
2:A93   Woodward, Ralph Lee. "Undergraduates and Latin American
           Studies: Latin American History Since Independence,"
           Secolas, vol. 2, no. 1 (1971), pp. 5-11.

B. SECONDARY SCHOOL

2:B1   Allen, Rodney F., and Joseph L. Fitzpatrick. "Using Poetry to
         Vitalize History," *Social Education*, vol. 29, no. 8 (1965),
         pp. 529-531, 533.

2:B2   Anthony, Albert S. "Pedagogical Limitations of the Source
         Materials Approach to the Teaching of History," *Social
         Studies*, vol. 60, no. 2 (1969), pp. 51-56.

2:B3   Atkinson, Michael C. "The Secondary School Syllabus," *Teach-
         ing History*, vol. 2, no. 4 (1970), pp. 288-291.

2:B4   Auerbach, F. *The Power of Prejudice in South African Educa-
         tion: An Enquiry into History Textbooks and Syllabuses in
         the Transvaal High Schools of South Africa.* Cape Town: A. A.
         Balkema, 1965.

2:B5   Barcan, Alan. *Social Science, History and the New Curriculum.*
         Sydney: Hicks Smith for Workers' Educational Association
         of N.S.W., 1971.

2:B6   Barr, Robert D. "Chaos and Contradiction: The Future of
         History in the Public Schools," *Social Studies*, vol. 59, no. 6
         (1968), pp. 257-260.

2:B7   Blyth, Joan E. "Archives and Source Material in the Junior
         School," *Teaching History*, vol. 1, no. 1 (1969), pp. 24-30.

2:B8   Boyce, Arnold Napier. *Teaching History in South African
         Schools.* Cape Town: Juta, 1968.

2:B9   British Parliamentary Group for World Government. *Cyprus
         School History Textbooks; A Study in Education for Inter-
         national Misunderstanding.* Extracts from Greek and Turkish
         school history textbooks used in Cyprus, translated by Barbara
         Hodge and Dr. G. L. Lewis, introduction by Prof. J. A.
         Lauwerys. London: Parliamentary Group for World Govern-
         ment, 1966.

2:B10   Brooks, Geoffrey Raymond. *A Select List of Aids of Use in the
         Teaching of Recent History.* London: Historical Association,
         1971.

2:B11   Brown, Godfrey N. *Living History: A Guide for Teachers in
         Africa.* London: Allen & Unwin, 1967.

2:B12   Buckwald, Joel. "Aims in Teaching World History," *Social
         Studies*, vol. 59, no. 4 (1968), pp. 164-166.

2:B13   Cambridge History Teaching Today Group. *The Teaching of History to the 11-14 Age Group: The Report of an Enquiry.* Cambridge: Cambridge Institute of Education, 1970.

2:B14   Carlson, Don M. "A United States History Course for Accelerated Students," *Social Studies,* vol. 59, no. 7 (1968), pp. 307-310.

2:B15   Cartwright, William H. "Brainwashing and the American Revolution," *Social Education,* vol. 29, no. 1 (1965), pp. 32-34.

2:B16   ———. "Selection, Organization, Presentation, and Placement of Subject Matter in American History," *Social Education,* vol. 29, no. 7 (1965), pp. 435-444, 463.

2:B17   Catchpole, Brian. *A Map History of the Modern World: 1890 to the Present Day.* London: Heinemann Educational, 1968.

2:B18   Cole, Donald B. *Preparation of Secondary-School History Teacher.* Donald B. Cole and Thomas Pressly for the American Historical Association's Committee on Teaching. 2nd edition. Washington, 1968.

2:B19   Coltham, Jeanette B. *Educational Objectives for the Study of History: A Suggested Framework,* by Jeanette B. Coltham, in collaboration with John Fines. London: Historical Association, 1971.

2:B20   Commager, Henry Steele. *The Nature and the Study of History.* With a Concluding Chapter Suggesting Methods for Elementary and Secondary Teachers by Raymond H. Muessig and Vincent R. Rogers. Columbus, Ohio: C. E. Merrill Books, 1965.

2:B21   ———. "Why History," *American Education,* vol. 1, no. 6 (1965), pp. 26-29.

2:B22   Conference on History in the Secondary School. *History in the Secondary School: The Report of a Conference Held on Friday 6th January, 1967, at the College of Preceptors and in the Swedenborg Hall.* London: Historical Association, 1967.

2:B23   Conference on the Utilization of Archival and Educational Resources. *Conference on the Utilization of Archival and Educational Resources: Proceedings.* Sacramento: Telefact Foundation, 1967.

2:B24   Conly, Dale L. "Senior Seminar: 'The Lost Generation,'" *New*

England Social Studies Bulletin, vol. 22, no. 2 (1965), pp. 28-33.

2:B25   Conrad, Edna. *History on the Stage: Children Make Plays from Historical Novels,* by Edna Conrad and Mary Van Dyke. New York: Van Nostrand Reinhold Co., 1971.

2:B26   Cordier, Ralph W. "The Study of History Through State and Local Resources," *Social Studies,* vol. 60, no. 3 (1969), pp. 99-104.

2:B27   Crookall, Robert Egerton. *Handbook for History Teachers in Africa.* 2nd ed. London: Evans Bros., 1972.

2:B28   Dance, E. H. *The Place of History in Secondary Teaching: A Comparative Study.* London: Harrap, 1970.

2:B29   Diadichenko, Vadym Arkhypovych. *Development of Historical Science in the Ukrainian SSR,* by V. A. Dyadichenko, F. E. Los and V. G. Sarbey. Kiev: Naukova Dumka, 1970.

2:B30   Dimond, Stanley E. "Social Studies in French Secondary Schools," *Social Education,* vol. 30, no. 3 (1966), pp. 175-178.

2:B31   Docking, James W. "History and the C.S.E.," *Teaching History,* vol. 1, no. 4 (1970), pp. 292-296.

2:B32   Douch, Robert. "Local History in School," *Amateur Historian,* vol. 6, no. 7 (1965), pp. 218-222.

2:B33   Draves, David D. "What's Wrong With the Teaching of History in the High School," *Social Studies,* vol. 56, no. 1 (1965), pp. 103-106.

2:B34   Dunner, Joseph, ed. *Handbook of World History: Concepts and Issues.* New York: Philosophical Library, 1967.

2:B35   Engle, Shirley. "World History in the Curriculum," *Social Education,* vol. 29, no. 7 (1965), pp. 459-463.

2:B36   Erickson, Edgar L. "A Case for English History," *Social Education,* vol. 29, no. 3 (1965), pp. 164-168.

2:B37   Estrin, Jack C. *World History Made Simple.* Revised edition. Garden City, N.Y.: Doubleday, 1968.

2:B38   Fairley, John Allan. *Activity Methods in History.* Illustrations by Marjorie F. Dixon. London: Nelson, 1967.

2:B39   Faissler, Margareta. *Key to the Past: Some History Books for Pre-College Readers.* 3rd edition. Washington: Service Center for Teachers of History, American Historical Association, 1965.

2:B40   Feder, Bernard, and Wallace K. Schoenberg. *High School World History Review Notes.* New York: Distributed by Monarch Press, 1964.

2:B41   Feldmesser, Robert A., and Paul E. Kelley. "Sociology and the Teaching of American History," *New England Social Studies Bulletin,* vol. 22, no. 2 (1965), pp. 8-14.

2:B42   Fendelman, Earl B., and Stephen N. Weideger. "American Studies: A Course in History and Literature for High School," *New England Social Studies Bulletin,* vol. 22, no. 2 (1965), pp. 21-26.

2:B43   Fenton, Edwin. "History in the New Social Studies," *Social Education,* vol. 30, no. 5 (1966), pp. 325-328.

2:B44   Ferguson, Sheila. *Projects in History for the Secondary School.* London: Batsford, 1967.

2:B45   Fines, John. "Archives in School," *History,* vol. 53, no. 179 (1968), pp. 348-356.

2:B46   ————. *The History Teacher and Other Disciplines.* London: Historical Association, 1970.

2:B47   ————. "Recent Research into the Teaching of History," *Teaching History,* vol. 1, no. 2 (1969), pp. 83-86.

2:B48   Fraenkel, Jack R. "Generalizations and the Teaching of History in the Secondary Schools," *California Social Science Review,* vol. 5, no. 1 (1965), pp. 14-20.

2:B49   Frédéricq, Paul. *The Study of History in England and Scotland.* Authorized translation from the French by Henrietta Leonard. New York: Johnson Reprint Corp., 1973 [1887].

2:B50   ————. *The Study of History in Holland and Belgium.* Authorized translation from the French by Henrietta Leonard. New York: Johnson Reprint Corp., 1973 [1890].

2:B51   Frerichs, Allen H. "Teachers, History, and Slow Learning Adolescents," *Social Studies,* vol. 58, no. 4 (1967), pp. 168-170.

2:B52   Gall, Morris. "The Future of History," *Social Education,* vol. 29, no. 5 (1965), pp. 269-271.

2:B53   Goergeoff, John. "The Writing of Historical Fiction: A Technique for Teaching History," *Social Studies,* vol. 56, no. 5 (1965), pp. 182-187.

2:B54   Gilliom, Eugene M. "Structure and the History Curriculum,"

Social Studies, vol. 59, no. 2 (1968), pp. 70-76.

2:B55   Good, John M. "Every Man His Own Historian," *California
         Social Science Review,* vol. 4, no. 3 (1965), pp. 17-21.

2:B56   Gosden, P. H. J. H. *History for the Average Child: Suggestions
         on Teaching History to Pupils of Average and Below Average
         Ability,* by P. H. J. H. Gosden and D. W. Sylvester. Oxford:
         Blackwell, 1968.

2:B57   Greever, Janet G., and Charles E. P. Simmons. "Latin American
         History: Suggestions for Junior and Senior High Schools,"
         Social Studies, vol. 58, no. 4 (1967), pp. 153-158.

2:B58   Griffiths, Naomi Elizabeth Saundaus. *Studying History: A Prac-
         tical Handbook.* London: Methuen, 1966.

2:B59   Great Britain. *Towards World History.* London: H. M. S. O.,
         1967.

2:B60   Hadkins, Lora. "The Bias in Teaching Boer War History," *Pat-
         terns of Prejudice,* vol. 5, no. 3 (1971), pp. 11-14.

2:B61   Hales, E. E. Y. "School History in the Melting Pot," *History
         Today,* vol. 16, no. 3 (1966), pp. 202-209.

2:B62   Halsey, Van R., Jr. "Frontal Attack on Pre-Canned History,"
         New England Social Studies Bulletin, vol. 22, no. 2 (1965),
         pp. 15-20.

2:B63   *Handbook for History Teachers.* 2nd ed. rewritten and enlarged.
         General editors: W. H. Burston and C. W. Green. London:
         Methuen Educational, 1970 [1962].

2:B64   Hantula, James. "The Heart of the Matter," *Social Studies,* vol.
         62, no. 6 (1971), pp. 248-252.

2:B65   Happer, Eric and Joan E. Blyth. "Model Making as an Approach
         to Local History in the Middle School," *Teaching History,*
         vol. 1, no. 3 (1970), pp. 158-163.

2:B66   Hardwick, Francis C. *Teaching History and Geography: A
         Source Book of Suggestions.* Assisted by Edith Deyell, J.
         Neil Sutherland and George S. Tomkins. Additional material
         from Neville V. Scarfe and others. 2nd edition. Toronto:
         W. J. Gage, 1967.

2:B67   Hastie, Tom. *History After Four O'Clock: Some Suggestions
         for Those Concerned with School History Clubs.* London:
         Historical Association, 1971.

2:B68   Healy, David F. *Modern Imperialism: Changing Styles in*

Historical Interpretation. Washington: Service Center for
Teachers of History, 1967.

2:B69   Hepworth, Philip. *How to Find Out in History: A Guide to
Sources of Information for All.* Oxford, N.Y.: Pergamon,
1966.

2:B70   *History in the Sixth Form and in Higher Education: Report
of a Conference Held on Friday, January 3rd, 1969, at the
Institute of Education, University of London.* London:
Historical Association, 1969.

2:B71   Hogeboom, Willard. "The High School Teacher and the Field of
History," *Social Studies,* vol. 59, no. 6 (1968), pp. 254-256.

2:B72   Incorporated Association of Assistant Masters in Secondary
Schools. *The Teaching of History in Secondary Schools.*
(1956), 3d ed. Cambridge, England: University Press, 1965.

2:B73   Inglis, Kenneth Stanley. *The Study of History in Papua and New
Guinea: Inaugural Lecture.* Port Moresby: University of
Papua and New Guinea, 1967.

2:B74   International Federation of Teachers' Associations. *Congress of
Dublin 1968. The Teaching of Human Rights through History
and Social Studies.* Lausanne, Switzerland, 1968.

2:B75   Irwin, Leonard Bertram. *A Guide to Historical Reading: Non-
Fiction for the Use of Schools, Libraries, and the General
Reader.* 9th revised edition, Brooklawn, N.J.: McKinley Pub-
lishing, 1970.

2:B76   *Japan at the XIIth International Congress of Historical Sciences
in Vienna.* Edited by the Japanese National Committee of
Historical Sciences. Tokyo: Nihon Gakujutsu Shinkokai,
1965.

2:B77   Jones, Grace. "Archives in History Teaching: Some Problems,"
Teaching History, vol. 1, no. 3 (1970), pp. 188-192.

2:B78   Kathleen, Sister M. "Who Shall Teach History?" *Catholic Educational Review,* vol. 64, no. 3 (1966), pp. 168-173.

2:B79   Katz, Loren B. "Some Guidelines in Teaching American Negro
History," *Negro History Bulletin,* vol. 28, no. 8 (1965), pp.
190-191.

2:B80   Keller, Charles R. "A New History and the Social Sciences,"
New England Social Studies Bulletin, vol. 23, no. 2 (1966),
pp. 14-19.

2:B81   Krug, Mark A. "For a Fair Deal in the Teaching of Reconstruction History," *Social Education*, vol. 29, no. 1 (1965), pp. 7-14, 56.

2:B82   ———. *History and the Social Sciences: New Approaches to the Teaching of Social Studies*. Waltham, Mass.: Blaisdell Publishing, 1967.

2:B83   Ladenburg, Thomas. "Teaching the Prosperity and Depression Decades," *Social Studies*, vol. 56, no. 7 (1965), pp. 266-271.

2:B84   Leinwand, Gerald, and Daniel M. Feins. *Teaching History and the Social Studies in Secondary Schools*. New York: Pitman Publishing, 1968.

2:B85   Lindfors, Kenneth I. "Making the American Past Relevant: Pitfalls and Possibilities," *New England Social Studies Bulletin*, vol. 23, no. 1 (1966), pp. 26-28.

2:B86   Lloyd, E. R. "The Use of Historical Documents in Schools," *Amateur Historian*, vol. 7, no. 2 (1966), pp. 47-52.

2:B87   Logasa, Hannah. *Historical Fiction: Guide for Junior and Senior High Schools and Colleges, also for General Reader*. 9th revised and enlarged edition. Brooklawn, N.J.: McKinley Publishing, 1968.

2:B88   Lord, Donald C. "Paperbacks and the Teaching of American History," *Social Studies*, vol. 59, no. 3 (1968), pp. 109-112.

2:B89   Lowther, Lawrence, and Floyd Rodine. "History Teaching in the High School: A Brief Survey of Washington State," *Pacific Northwest Quarterly*, vol. 59, no. 3 (1968), pp. 147-155.

2:B90   MacIntosh, Henry Gordon. *The Construction and Analysis of an Objective Test in Ordinary Level History: A Report on Work Carried Out by the Associated Examining Board Between October 1967 and March 1969*. Aldershot (Hants.): Associated Examining Board, 1969.

2:B91   McMillan, N. A. C. *A New Certificate History*. London: University of London Press, 1966.

2:B92   Martorella, Peter H. "Carl Becker and Secondary Social Studies," *Social Studies*, vol. 58, no. 5 (1967), pp. 194-199.

2:B93   Meiburger, Anna. "The Technique of Comparison and Contrast in Teaching History," *Social Studies*, vol. 60, no. 5 (1969), pp. 201-204.

2:B94   Milburn, Geoffrey, comp. *Teaching History in Canada*. Toronto, New York: McGraw-Hill, Ryerson, 1972.

2:B95   Mississippi Department of Education, Division of Instruction.
        *World History: A Course of Study and Teaching Guide for
        Grade 10.* Jackson, 1968.
2:B96   Moorsom, Norman. "Local History in a Town School,"
        Amateur Historian, vol. 6, no. 7 (1965), pp. 225-227.
2:B97   Morgan, Edmund Sears. *So What About History?* New York:
        Atheneum, 1969.
2:B98   Mowat, C. L. "A Study of Bias in British and American
        History Textbooks," *British Association for American
        Studies Bulletin,* no. 10 (1965), pp. 31-39.
2:B99   Neyland, Leedell W. "Why Negro History in the Junior and
        Senior High Schools?" *Social Studies,* vol. 58, no. 7 (1967),
        pp. 315-321.
2:B100 Nield, Jonathan. *A Guide to the Best Historical Novels and
        Tales.* New York: B. Franklin, 1968.
2:B101 Northeast, Peter. "Local History in a Village School," *Amateur
        Historian,* vol. 6, no. 7 (1965), pp. 223-224.
2:B102 Pickens, William G. "Teaching Negro Culture in High Schools—
        Is It Worthwhile?," *Journal of Negro Education,* vol. 34,
        no. 2 (1965), pp. 106-113.
2:B103 Potdar, Datto Vaman. *The Place and Purpose of History in Our
        Education.* Ahmedabad: Harold Laski Institute of Political
        Science, 1962.
2:B104 Preston, Gillian. "The Value of Local History in the School
        Curriculum," *Teaching History,* vol. 1, no. 2 (1969), pp.
        87-91.
2:B105 Price, Mary. "History in Danger," *History,* vol. 53, no. 179
        (1968), pp. 342-347.
2:B106 Pundeff, Marin V., ed. *History in the U.S.S.R.: Selected Read-
        ings.* San Francisco: Published for the Hoover Institution
        on War, Revolution and Peace, Stanford University, Chandler
        Publishing, 1967.
2:B107 Rojas, Billy. "The End of History," *Social Studies,* vol. 63, no.
        3 (1972), pp. 118-124.
2:B108 Roots, David E. "An Investigation into the Use of Fieldwork
        in History Teaching," *Teaching History,* vol. 1, no. 4 (1970),
        pp. 269-271.
2:B109 Rosen, Philip. "Helping Students to Use Documents," *Social
        Studies,* vol. 57, no. 1 (1966), pp. 14-16.

2:B110   Rundell, Walter, Jr. "Clio's Ways and Means: A Preliminary
         Report on the Survey," *Historian*, vol. 30, no. 1 (1967),
         pp. 20-40.

2:B111   ———. "History Teaching: A Legitimate Concern," *Social
         Education*, vol. 29, no. 8 (1965), pp. 521-524, 528.

2:B112   Sachs, Stephen M. "The Uses and Limits of Simulation Models
         in Teaching Social Science and History," *Social Studies*,
         vol. 61, no. 4 (1970), pp. 163-167.

2:B113   School Broadcasting Council for the United Kingdom. *History
         and School Broadcasting*. London: British Broadcasting,
         1957.

2:B114   Schuddekopf, Otto Ernst, in collaboration with Edouard
         Bruley, E. H. Dance, and Haakon Vigander. *History Teach-
         ing and History Textbook Revision*. Strasbourg: Council
         for Cultural Co-operation of the Council of Europe, 1967.

2:B115   Seaberg, Stanley, and William Mulhair. "High School Students
         Test the Frontier Thesis," *Social Education*, vol. 29, no. 5
         (1965), pp. 279-280.

2:B116   Sellen, Robert W. "Boris, Figaro and Manrico: History Through
         Music," *History Teacher*, vol. 5, no. 2 (1972), pp. 48-52.

2:B117   Shropshire, Olive Estil. *The Teaching of History in English
         Schools*. New York: AMS Press, 1972 [1936].

2:B118   Spector, Robert M. "The Better Preparation of High School
         Students for Their College History Courses," *Social Studies*,
         vol. 58, no. 6 (1967), pp. 235-241.

2:B119   Stavrianos, L. S. "The Teaching of World History," *History
         Teacher*, vol. 3, no. 1 (1969), pp. 19-24.

2:B120   Steinkamp, John R. "The Demands on the History Teacher
         Using the Inquiry Method," *Social Studies*, vol. 61, no. 3
         (1970), pp. 195-198.

2:B121   Strong, Douglas H., and Elizabeth S. Rosenfield. "What Is
         History? A Neglected Question," *Social Studies*, vol. 59,
         no. 5 (1968), pp. 195-198.

2:B122   Swift, Donald C., and Rodney F. Allen. "History Instruction
         and Human Aspirations: A Proposed Synthesis," *Social
         Studies*, vol. 57, no. 1 (1966), pp. 3-7.

2:B123   Trezise, Robert L. "The Black American in American History
         Textbooks," *Social Studies*, vol. 60, no. 4 (1969), pp. 164-167.

2:B124   Trueman, John Herbert. *The Anatomy of History.* Toronto:
         J. M. Dent, 1967.
2:B125   Vajreswari, R. *A Handbook for History Teachers.* Bombay,
         New York: Allied Publishers, 1966.
2:B126   Wake, R. "History as a Separate Discipline: The Case," *Teaching History,* vol. 1, no. 3 (1970), pp. 153-157.
2:B127   Washington, E. S. "Report on an Experiment in History Teaching," *Teaching History,* vol. 1, no. 1 (1969), pp. 31-34.
2:B128   Watts, David George. *The Learning of History,* by D. G. Watts.
         London, Boston: Routledge and Kegan Paul, 1972.
2:B129   Wendel, Thomas. "In Defense of Early American History,"
         Social Studies, vol. 60, no. 1 (1969), pp. 3-11.
2:B130   White, Andrew Dickson. *European Schools of History and
         Politics.* New York: Johnson Reprint Corp., 1973 [1887].
2:B131   White, T. M. "Unifying the Study of American History and
         Literature," *Social Studies,* vol. 56, no. 2 (1965), pp. 48-51.
2:B132   Wilson, Norman H. "The New Social Studies: Understanding
         the Systems of War and Peace," *Social Studies,* vol. 60,
         no. 3 (1969), pp. 119-124.

3. HISTORIOGRAPHY AND PHILOSOPHY OF HISTORY

3:1   Abbott, Wilbur Cortez. *Adventures in Reputation: With an Essay on some New History and Historians.* Port Washington, N.Y.: Kennikat Press, 1969 [1935].

3:2   Acheson, Dean Gooderham. *History as Literature.* New York: McGraw-Hill, 1966.

3:3   Acton, John Emerich Edward Dalberg. *Essays in the Liberal Interpretation of History.* Introduction by William H. McNeil. Chicago: University of Chicago Press, 1967.

3:4   ———. *The History of Freedom, and Other Essays.* Edited with an introduction by John Neville Figgis and Reginald Vere Laurence. Freeport, N.Y.: Books for Libraries Press, 1967 [1907].

3:5   ———. *Historical Essays & Studies.* Edited by John Neville Figgis and Reginald Vere Laurence. Freeport, N.Y.: Books for Libraries Press, 1967 [1907].

3:6   Adams, Brooks. *The Law of Civilization and Decay: An Essay on History.* With an introduction by Charles A. Beard. New York: Books for Libraries Press, 1971 [c. 1943].

3:7   ———. *The New Empire, with an Appendix Containing a Chronological Survey from 4000 B.C. up till 1900.* New York: Bergman Publishers, 1969 [1902].

3:8   Adorno, T. W. "Was Spengler Right?," *Encounter,* vol. 26, no. 148 (1966), pp. 25-29.

3:9   Albrektson, Bertil. *History and the Gods: An Essay on the Idea of Historical Events as Divine Manifestations in the Ancient Near East and in Israel.* Lund: Gleerup, 1967.

3:10   Apter, David E. "Radicalization and Embourgeoisement: Some Hypotheses for a Comparative Study of History." *Journal of Interdisciplinary History,* vol. 1, no. 3 (1971), pp. 511-526.

3:11   Arendt, Hannah. *Between Past and Future: Eight Exercises in Political Thought.* Enlarged edition. New York: Viking Press, 1968.

3:12   Arthur, C. J. "On the Historical Understanding," *History and Theory,* vol. 7, no. 2 (1968), pp. 203-216.

3:13   Ashley, Maurice. "Churchill and History," *International Affairs*, vol. 42, no. 1 (1966), pp. 87-94.

3:14   Atherton, John. "Michelet: Three Conceptions of Historical Becoming," *Studies in Romanticism*, vol. 4, no. 4 (1965), pp. 220-239.

3:15   Ausubel, Herman. *Historians and Their Craft: A Study of the Presidential Address of the American Historical Association.* New York: Russell & Russell, 1950.

3:16   Ayala, Francisco J., et al. *Biology, History and Natural Philosophy.* Ed. by Allen D. Breck and Wolfgang Yourgrau. New York: Plenum Press, 1972.

3:17   Bahr, Hans Walter. "Past and Future as Problems of Modern Cultural Consciousness." *United Asia*, vol. 19, no. 6 (1967), pp. 418-423.

3:18   Balthasar, Hans Urs von. *Man in History: A Theological Study.* Translated from the German by William Glen-Doepel. London, Sydney: Sheed and Ward, 1968.

3:19   ———. *A Theological Anthropology.* New York: Sheed and Ward, 1967.

3:20   Banner, Lois W. "On Writing Women's History," *Journal of Interdisciplinary Studies*, vol. 2, no. 2 (1972), pp. 347-358.

3:21   Barnes, Harry Elmer. *History and Social Intelligence.* New York: Revisionist Press, 1972 [1926].

3:22   ———. *The New History and the Social Studies.* New York: Revisionist Press, 1972 [1925].

3:23   Barraclough, Geoffrey. *History and the Common Man: Presidential Address, Diamond Jubilee Conference, London, 12-16 April, 1966.* London: Historical Association, 1967.

3:24   Barzun, Jacques. "History: The Muse and Her Doctors," *American Historical Review*, vol. 77, no. 1 (1972), pp. 36-64.

3:25   Becker, Carl Lotus. *Everyman His Own Historian: Essays on History and Politics.* Chicago: Quadrangle Books, 1966.

3:26   Beidelman, T. O. "Levi-Strauss and History," *Journal of Interdisciplinary History*, vol. 1, no. 3 (1971), pp. 511-526.

3:27   Bell, J. H., and J. R. von Sturmer. "Claude Levi-Straus: Social Anthropology and History," *Australian Journal of Politics and History*, vol. 16, no. 2 (1970), pp. 218-226.

3:28   Beloff, Max. "On Thinking About the Past," *Encounter*, vol. 33, no. 192 (1969), pp. 43-51.

3:29 Bennis, Warren G. "Future of the Social Sciences," *Antioch Review,* vol. 28, no. 2 (1968), pp. 227-255.

3:30 Berkhof, Hendrikus. *Christ and the Meaning of History.* Translated by Lambertus Buurman. Richmond: John Knox Press, 1966.

3:31 Berlin, Isaiah. *The Hedgehog and the Fox: An Essay on Tolstoy's View of History.* London: Weidenfeld & Nicolson, 1967 [1953].

3:32 Bernstein, Barton J., ed. *Towards a New Past: Dissenting Essays in American History.* New York: Random House, 1967.

3:33 Biddiss, Michael D. "Prophecy and Pragmatism: Gobineau's Confrontation with Tocqueville," *Historical Journal,* vol. 13, no. 4 (1970), pp. 611-633.

3:34 Bietenholz, Peter G. *History and Biography in the Work of Erasmus of Rotterdam.* Geneve: Droz, 1966.

3:35 *Biology, History and Natural Philosophy.* Edited by Allen D. Breck and Wolfgang Yourgrau. New York: Plenum Press, 1972.

3:36 Black, John Bennett. *The Art of History: A Study of Four Great Historians of the Eighteenth Century.* New York: Russell & Russell, 1965.

3:37 Blondel, Maurice. *The Letter on Apologetics and History and Dogma.* Texts presented and translated by Alexander Dru and Illtyd Tretnowan. New York: Holt, Rinehart and Winston, 1965.

3:38 Boardman, Fon Wyman. *History and Historians.* New York: H. Z. Walck, 1965.

3:39 Bodin, Jean. *Method for the Easy Comprehension of History.* Translated by Beatrice Reynolds. New York: Octagon Books, 1966 [1945].

3:40 Bolingbroke, Henry Saint-John, 1st Viscount. *Letters on the Study and Use of History.* 2 vols. New York: Garland Publishing, 1970.

3:41 Borsodi, Ralph. *Seventeen Problems of Man and Society.* Anand: Charotar Book Stall, 1968.

3:42 Boulding, Kenneth E. *A Primer on Social Dynamics: History as Dialectics and Development.* New York: Free Press, 1970, pp. viii, 153.

3:43 Bourke, Paul F. "A Note on Historicism: Beard, Meinecke and

Collingwood," *Clio,* vol. 2, no. 1 (1972), pp. 65-69.

3:44 Braaten, Carl E. *History and Hermeneutics.* Philadelphia: Westminster Press, 1966.

3:45 Bradley, Francis Herbert. *The Presuppositions of Critical History.* Edited with introduction and commentary by Lionel Rubinoff. Don Mills, Ont.: J. M. Dent, 1968.

3:46 Brandon, Samuel George Frederick. *History, Time and Deity: A Historical and Comparative Study of the Conception of Time in Religious Thought and Practice.* Manchester: Manchester University Press, New York: Barnes & Noble, 1965.

3:47 Braybrooke, David. "Refinements of Culture in Large Scale History." *History and Theory,* beiheft 9 (1969), pp. 39-63.

3:48 Brenner, Robert Hamless, ed. *Essays on History and Literature,* by Daniel Aaron and others. Columbus: Ohio State University Press, 1966.

3:49 Buel, Richard, Jr. "Politics, Language and Time: Essays on Political Thought and History," *History and Theory,* vol. 12, no. 2 (1973), pp. 251-264.

3:50 Burridge, K. O. L. " 'Culture and Personality' and History: A Review," *Journal of World History,* vol. 9, no. 1 (1965), pp. 15-29.

3:51 Burrow, John Wyon. *Evolution and Society: A Study in Victorian Social Theory.* London: Cambridge University Press, 1966.

3:52 Bury, John Bagnell. *Selected Essays.* Harold Temperley, ed. Freeport, N.Y.: Books for Libraries Press, 1968.

3:53 Butterfield, Sir Herbert. *The Discontinuities between the Generations in History: Their Effect on the Transmission of Political Experience.* The Rede Lecture, 1971. New York: Cambridge University Press, 1972.

3:54 ———. *Man on His Past: The Study of the History of Historical Scholarship.* London: Cambridge University Press, 1969 [1955].

3:55 ———. "Narrative History and the Spade-Work Behind It," *History,* vol. 53, no. 178 (1968), pp. 165-180.

3:56 ———. *The Present State of Historical Scholarship: An Inaugural Lecture.* Cambridge, Eng.: University Press, 1965.

3:57 Campa, Arthur L. "Folklore and History," *Western Folklore,* vol. 24, no. 1 (1965), pp. 1-6.

3:58 Canning, John, ed. *100 Great Events that Changed the World from Babylonia to the Space Age.* London: Odhams, 1966.
3:59 Cardan, Paul. *History and Revolution: A Revolutionary Critique of Historical Materialism.* Bromley: Solidarity, 1971.
3:60 Carr, Herbert Wildon. *The Philosophy of Benedetto Croce: the Problem of Art and History.* New York: Russell & Russell, 1969.
3:61 Casserly, Julian Victor Langmead. *Toward a Theology of History.* New York: Holt, Rinehart and Winston, 1965.
3:62 *The Catholic Philosophy of History.* Peter Guilday, ed. Introduction by Ross J. S. Hoffman. Freeport, N.Y.: Books for Libraries Press, 1967.
3:63 Chaadaev, Petr Iakovlevich. *Philosophical Letters, and Apology of a Madman.* Translated with an introduction by Mary-Barbara Zeldin. Knoxville: University of Tennessee Press, 1969.
3:64 Chadwick, Owen. *Freedom and the Historian: An Inaugural Lecture.* London: Cambridge University Press, 1969.
3:65 Chambers, Lenoir, Virginius Dabney, and David J. Mays. "History as an Avocation," *Virginia Magazine of History and Biography,* vol. 76, no. 2 (1968), pp. 131-145.
3:66 *Changing Perspectives on Man.* Ben Rothblatt, ed. Chicago: University of Chicago Press, 1968.
3:67 Chattopadhyaya, Debiprasad. *Individuals and Societies, a Methodological Inquiry.* Bombay, N.Y.: Allied Publishers, 1967.
3:68 Chifflot, T. G. *Approaches to a Theology of History.* Translated from French by Mary Perkins Ryan. New York: Desclee Co., 1965.
3:69 Clark, C. M. H. "The Writing of History," *Victorian Historical Magazine,* vol. 39 (1968), pp. 151-152, pp. 11-23.
3:70 Clive, John. *Macaulay: The Shaping of a Historian.* N.Y.: Knopf, 1973.
3:71 Coblentz, Stanton Arthur. *Ten Crises in Civilization.* Chicago: Follett Pub., 1965.
3:72 Cochrane, Charles Norris. *Thucydides and the Science of History.* New York: Russell & Russell, 1965.
3:73 Cochrane, Thomas C. "History and Cultural Crisis," *American Historical Review,* vol. 78, no. 1 (1973), pp. 1-10.

3:74   Colacurcio, Michael. "The Dynamo and the Angelic Doctor: The Bias of Henry Adams' Medievalism," *American Quarterly,* vol. 17, no. 4 (1965), pp. 696-712.

3:75   Colby, Elbridge. "Roads of Research Beyond the Books," *Military Affairs,* vol. 31, no. 2 (1967), pp. 91-93.

3:76   Cole, C. Robert. "Intellectual History and the Common Man," *Rocky Mountain Social Science Journal,* vol. 9, no. 3 (1972), pp. 45-46.

3:77   Collingwood, Robin George. *Essays in the Philosophy of History.* Edited with Introduction by William Debbins. Austin: University of Texas Press, 1965.

3:78   Collis, Maurice. *The Journey Up: Reminiscences, 1934-1968.* London: Faber, 1970.

3:79   Commager, Henry Steele. "The Americanization of History," *Saturday Review,* November 1, vol. 52 (1969), pp. 24-25.

3:80   Conkin, Paul K. *The Heritage and Challenge of History.* N.Y.: Dodd, Mead and Company, 1971.

3:81   Connolly, James M. *Human History and the Word of God: The Christian Meaning of History in Contemporary Thought.* New York: Macmillan, 1965.

3:82   Cooke, Raymond M. "The Historian as Underdog: Eric Williams and the British Empire," *History,* vol. 33, no. 4 (1971), pp. 596-610.

3:83   Constantinescu, Miron, and Vasile Liveanu. *Problems of History and of Social Theory.* Trans. by Mary Lazarescu. Bibliotheca Historica Romaniae, Studies, no. 30. Bucharest: Publishing House of the Academy of the Socialist Republic of Romania, 1970.

3:84   Crawford, R. M. "The Practice of History: Thoughts on Reading Elton, Hancock, and Stretton," *Historical Studies,* vol. 14, no. 54 (1970), pp. 261-272.

3:85   Creighton, Mandell. *Historical Lectures and Addresses.* Edited by Louise Creighton. Freeport, N.Y.: Books for Libraries Press, 1967.

3:86   Croce, Benedetto. *Historical Materialism and the Economics of Karl Marx.* Translated by C. M. Meredith, introduction by A. D. Lindsay. New York: Russell & Russell, 1966 [1914].

3:87   ————. *History as the Story of Liberty.* Translated by Silvia Sprigge. Chicago: Regnery, 1970 [1931].

3:88   ———. *Philosophy, Poetry, History: An Anthology of Essays.* Translated from the Italian, and introduced by Cecil Sprigge. London, New York: Oxford University Press, 1966.

3:89   Cromer, Evelyn Baring. *Political and Literary Essays, 1908-1913.* Freeport, N.Y.: Books for Libraries Press, 1969.

3:90   Cronin, Richard J. "The Theology of History," *Philippine Studies,* vol. 13, no. 3 (1965), pp. 687-705.

3:91   Cullman, Oscar. *Salvation in History.* English translation drafted by Sidney G. Sowers and afterwards completed by editorial staff of SCM Press. 1st American edition. New York: Harper & Row, 1967.

3:92   Cuneo, Ernest. *Science and History.* New York: Duell, Sloan and Pearce, 1968.

3:93   Danto, Arthur Coleman. *Analytical Philosophy of History.* Cambridge: Cambridge University Press, 1968.

3:94   Davis, David B. "Some Recent Directions in Cultural History," *American Historical Review,* vol. 73, no. 3 (1968), pp. 696-707.

3:95   Dawson, Christopher. *Progress and Religion: An Historical Enquiry.* Westport, Conn.: Greenwood Press, 1970.

3:96   Deluz-Chiva, Ariane. "Anthropology, History and Historiography," *International Social Science Journal,* vol. 17, no. 4 (1965), pp. 571-581.

3:97   Destler, Chester McArthur. "The Crocean Origin of Becker's Historical Relativism," *History and Theory,* vol. 9, no. 3 (1970), pp. 335-342.

3:98   Deva, Indra. "The Course of Social Change: A Hypothesis," *Diogenes,* vol. 56 (1966), pp. 74-91.

3:99   Dietl, Paul J. "Deduction and Historical Explanation," *History and Theory,* vol. 7, no. 2 (1968), pp. 167-188.

3:100   Dilthey, Wilhelm. *Pattern and Meaning in History: Thoughts on History and Society.* Edited with introduction by H. P. Richman. New York: Harper & Row, 1971 [1961].

3:101   Donagan, Alan and Barbara Donagan. *Philosophy of History.* New York: Macmillan, 1965.

3:102   Donald, David. "Between Science and Art," *American Historical Review,* vol. 77, no. 2 (1972), pp. 445-452.

3:103   ———. "Radical Historians on the Move," *The New York Times Book Review,* July 19, 1970, sec. 7, pp. 1-2.

3:104 Dovring, Folke. "The Principle of Acceleration: A Non-Dialectical Theory of Progress," *Comparative Studies in Society and History,* vol. 11, no. 4 (1969), pp. 413-425.

3:105 Downing, F. Gerald. "Philosophy of History and Historical Research," *Philosophy,* vol. 44, no. 165 (1969), pp. 33-45.

3:106 Dozer, Donald M. "History as Force," *Pacific Historical Review,* vol. 34, no. 4 (1965), pp. 375-395.

3:107 Dray, W. H. "On the Nature and Role of Narrative in Historiography," *History and Theory,* vol. 10, no. 2 (1971), pp. 153-171.

3:108 ———. "The Politics of Contemporary Philosophy of History: A Reply to Hayden White," *Clio,* vol. 3, no. 1 (1973), pp. 55-76.

3:109 ———, ed. *Philosophical Analysis and History.* New York: Harper & Row, 1966.

3:110 Duberman, Martin, "The Limitations of History," *Antioch Review,* vol. 25, no. 2 (1965), pp. 283-296.

3:111 ———. *The Uncompleted Past.* New York: Random House, 1969.

3:112 Dunn, John. "The Identity of the History of Ideas," *Philosophy,* vol. 43, no. 164 (1968), pp. 85-104.

3:113 Dunning, William A. *Truth in History and Other Essays.* Port Washington, N.Y.: Kennikat Press, 1965.

3:114 Durant, William James and Ariel Durant. *The Lessons of History.* New York: Simon and Schuster, 1968.

3:115 Ebeling, Gerhard. *The Problem of Historicity in the Church and Its Proclamation.* Translated by Grover Foley. Philadelphia: Fortress Press, 1967.

3:116 Eckstein, Harry. "On the Etiology of Internal Wars," *History and Theory,* vol. 4, no. 2 (1965), pp. 133-163.

3:117 Eisenstein, Elizabeth. "Clio and Chronos: An Essay on the Making and Breaking of History-Book Time," *History and Theory,* beiheft 6 (1966), pp. 36-64.

3:118 Ellison, Ralph, et al. "The Uses of History in Fiction," *Southern Literary Journal,* vol. 1, no. 2 (1969), pp. 57-90.

3:119 Ely, Richard, Rolf Gruner, and William Dray. "Mandelbaum on Historical Narrative: A Discussion," *History and Theory,* vol. 8, no. 3 (1969), pp. 275-294.

3:120   English, John C. "Existentialism and the Study of History,"
        Social Science, vol. 41, no. 3 (1966), pp. 153-160.

3:121   *Essays in History: Presented to Reginald Lane Poole.* H. W. C.
        Davis, ed. Oxford: Clarendon Press, 1969.

3:122   *Essays in History and Political Theory in Honor of Charles
        Howard Mellwain.* Carl Wittke, ed. New York: Russell &
        Russell, 1936.

3:123   *Essays in Intellectual History.* Dedicated to James Harvey
        Robinson by his Former Seminar Students. New York: AMS
        Press, 1973 [1929].

3:124   Fain, Haskell. *Between Philosophy and History: The Resurrec-
        tion of Speculative Philosophy of History Within the Analytic
        Tradition.* Princeton, N.J.: Princeton University Press, 1970.

3:125   ———. "History as Science," *History and Theory,* vol. 9,
        no. 2 (1970), pp. 154-173.

3:126   Farmer, W., ed. *Christian History and Interpretation.* Fest-
        schrift for J. Knox. Cambridge: Cambridge University Press,
        1967.

3:127   Farrell, John K. A. "H. G. Wells as an Historian," *University of
        Windsor Review,* vol. 2, no. 2 (1967), pp. 47-57.

3:128   Febvre, Lucian Paul Victor. *A New Kind of History: From the
        Writings of Febvre.* Edited by Peter Burke, translated from
        the French by K. Folca. London: Routledge and Kegan Paul,
        1973.

3:129   Feis, Herbert. "The Prankishness of History," *Virginia Quarterly
        Review,* vol. 41, no. 1 (1965), pp. 58-66.

3:130   Fell, Albert Prior, comp. *Historians and Historians: A Selection
        of Articles from History Today.* Edited with an original intro-
        ductory essay by Albert Prior Fell. Edinburgh, London: Oliver
        & Boyd, 1968.

3:131   Feuer, Lewis S. "Karl Marx and the Promethean Complex,"
        Encounter, vol. 31, no. 183 (1968), pp. 15-32.

3:132   Firda, Richard Arthur. "German Philosophy of History and
        Literature in the *North American Review:* 1815-1860,"
        Journal of the History of Ideas, vol. 32, no. 1 (1971), pp.
        133-142.

3:133   Fischer, David Hackett. *Historians' Fallacies: Toward a Logic of
        Historical Thought.* New York: Harper & Row, 1970.

3:134 Fisher, Herbert Albert Laurens. *Studies in History and Politics.*
       Freeport, N.Y.: Books for Libraries Press, 1967.
3:135 Fitzsimons, Matthew A., Alfred G. Pundt and Charles E. Nowell,
       eds. *The Development of Historiography.* Port Washington,
       N.Y.: Kennikat Press, 1967 [1954].
3:136 Flechtheim, Ossip Kurt. *History and Futurology.* With a fore-
       word by Robert Jungk. Meisenheim am Glan: Hain, 1966.
3:137 Fleischer, Helmut. *Marxism and History.* Translated from the
       German by Eric Mosbacher. London: Allen Lane, 1973.
3:138 Fleishman, Robert W. "On the Problem of 'National Personality'
       in Historical Writing," *Duquesne Review,* vol. 12, no. 1 (1967),
       pp. 23-33.
3:139 Flender, Helmut. *St. Luke: Theologian of Redemptive History.*
       Translated by R. Ruller. Philadelphia: Fortress Press, 1967.
3:140 Flint, Robert. *The Philosophy of History in France and Germany.*
       Geneve: Slatkine Reprints, 1971 [1874].
3:141 *For Hilaire Belloc: Essays in Honor of his 71st Birthday.* Douglas
       Woodruff, ed. New York: Greenwood Press, 1969 [1942].
3:142 Freeman, Edward Augustus. *Historical Essays.* New York: AMS
       Press, 1969.
3:143 Fromm, Harold. "Emerson and Kierkegaard: The Problem of
       Historical Christianity," *Massachusetts Review,* vol. 9, no. 4
       (1968), pp. 741-752.
3:144 Furet, Francois. "Quantitative History," *Daedalus,* vol. 100, no. 1
       (1971), pp. 151-167.
3:145 Galbraith, John S. "Some Reflections on the Profession of
       History," *Pacific Historical Review,* vol. 35, no. 1 (1966), pp.
       1-13.
3:146 Gallis, W. B. *Philosophy and Historical Understanding.* 2d ed.
       New York: Schocken Books, 1968.
3:147 Gardiner, Patrick. *The Nature of Historical Explanation.* London,
       New York: Oxford University Press, 1968.
3:148 Gawronski, Donald V. *History: Meaning and Method.* Consult-
       ing ed.: Russel B. Nye. Revised edition. Glenview, Ill: Scott,
       Foresman, 1969.
3:149 Gay, Peter. *The Bridge of Criticism.* Harper Torchbooks. New
       York: Harper & Row, 1970.
3:150 ———, and Gerald J. Cavanaugh, eds. *Historians at Work.* In
       2 vols. New York: Harper & Row, 1972.

3:151 ———, comp. *Historians at Work.* Edited by Peter Gay and
        Gerald J. Cavanaugh. New York: Harper & Row, 1972.
3:152 ———. "The History of History," *Horizon,* vol. 11, no. 4
        (1969), pp. 112-119.
3:153 Gellner, Ernest. "Our Current Sense of History," *Survey,* vol.
        17, no. 3 (1971), pp. 13-30.
3:154 "A General Theory of Innovations," *Comparative Studies in
        History and Society,* vol. 11 (1969), pp. 369-432.
3:155 Gentles, Frederick, and Melvin Steinfeld. *Hangups from Way
        Back: Historical Myths and Canons.* San Francisco: Canfield
        Press, 1970.
3:156 Geyl, Pieter. *Use and Abuse of History.* Hamden, Conn.:
        Archon Books, 1970 [1955].
3:157 Gilb, Corinne Lathrop. "Time and Change in Twentieth Century
        Thought," *Journal of World History,* vol. 9, no. 4 (1966),
        pp. 867-880.
3:158 Gilbert, Arthur N., comp. *In Search of a Meaningful Past.*
        Boston: Houghton Mifflin Co., 1971.
3:159 Gillespie, Neal C. "George Frederick Holmes and the Philosophy
        of History," *South Atlantic Quarterly,* vol. 67, no. 3 (1968),
        pp. 436-498.
3:160 Glezerman, G. "V. I. Lenin and the Problems of Scientific
        Prevision," *Communist Viewpoint,* vol. 2, no. 5 (1970), pp.
        28-38.
3:161 Goddard, David. "Max Weber and the Objectivity of Social
        Science," *History and Theory,* vol. 12, no. 1 (1973), pp. 1-22.
3:162 Goel, Dharmendra. *Philosophy of History: A Critical Study of
        Recent Philosophies of History.* Delhi: Sterling Publishers,
        1967.
3:163 Goldstein, Leon J. "Collingwood on Historical Knowing,"
        History and Theory, vol. 9, no. 1 (1970), pp. 3-36.
3:164 Gooch, George Peabody. *Historical Surveys and Portraits.* New
        York: Barnes & Noble, 1966.
3:165 ———. *History and Historians in the Nineteenth Century.*
        Boston: Beacon Press, 1965 [1913].
3:166 ———. *Maria Theresa, and other Studies.* Hamden, Conn.:
        Archon Books, 1965 [1952].
3:167 Gore, John. "Clio in No Hurry," *Quarterly Review,* vol. 304,
        no. 650 (1966), pp. 414-418.

3:168   Gould, J. B. "Hypothetical History," *Economic History Review,* vol. 22, no. 2 (1969), pp. 195-207.

3:169   Graham, Gerald Sandford and John Alexander. *The Secular Abyss: An Interpretation of History and the Human Situation.* Wheaton, Ill.: Theosophical Pub. House, 1967.

3:170   Grant, George Parkin. *Time as History.* Toronto: Canadian Broadcasting Corp., 1969.

3:171   Gray, J. M. "Biography as History," *Canadian Historical Association Annual Report* (1965), pp. 144-153.

3:172   Grimes, Howard. *The Christian Views History.* Nashville: Published for the Cooperative Publication Association by Abingdon Press, 1969.

3:173   Gruner, Rolf. "Ranke's Historical Theory," *Durham University Journal,* vol. 59, no. 3 (1967), pp. 139-144.

3:174   Grunfeld, Joseph. "Historical Insight," *Revue de l'Université d'Ottawa,* vol. 38, no. 1 (1968), pp. 73-96.

3:175   Gunnell, John G. *Political Philosophy and Time.* Middletown, Conn.: Wesleyan University Press, 1968.

3:176   Halle, Louis J. "A Multitude of Cold Wars," *International Journal,* vol. 23, no. 3 (1968), pp. 335-343.

3:177   ———. "What is Contemporary History?" *Virginia Quarterly Review,* vol. 43, no. 4 (1967), pp. 566-579.

3:178   Halvorson, John V. *The Ages in Tension.* Minneapolis: Augsburg Pub. House, 1970.

3:179   Hampson, Norman. *History as an Art: An Inaugural Lecture Delivered Before the University of Newcastle upon Tyne on Monday, 19 February, 1968.* Newcastle upon Tyne: University of Newcastle upon Tyne, 1968.

3:180   Handlin, Oscar. "History: A Discipline in Crisis?," *American Scholar,* vol. 40, no. 3 (1971), pp. 447-465.

3:181   Harder, Helmut G., and W. Taylor Stevenson. "The Continuity of History and Faith in the Theology of Wolfhart Pannenberg: Toward an Erotics of History," *Journal of Religion,* vol. 51, no. 1 (1971), pp. 34-56.

3:182   Harvey, Van Austin. *The Historian and the Believer: The Morality of Historical Knowledge and Christian Belief.* New York: Macmillan, 1966.

3:183   Haye, Kh. A. *Great Lives.* Karachi: Patwa Printers, 1966.

3:184   Hayner, Paul Collins. *Reason and Existence: Schelling's Philos-
        ophy of History.* LeMen: F. J. Brill, 1967.
3:185   Hefner, Philip J. *Faith and the Vitalities of History: A Theological
        Study Based on the Work of Albrecht Ritschl.* New York:
        Harper & Row, 1966.
3:186   Heilbronner, Robert. "Do Machines Make History?," *Technology
        and Culture,* vol. 8, no. 3 (1967), pp. 335-345.
3:187   Hein, Steven A. "The Christian Historian: Apologist or Seeker?
        A Reply to Ronald J. VanderMolen," *Fiedes et Historicum,*
        vol. 4 (Spring, 1972), pp. 85-93.
3:188   Herder, Johann Gottfried von. *J. G. Herder and Social and
        Political Culture.* Translated, edited and with an introduction
        by F. M. Barnard. London: Cambridge University Press, 1969.
3:189   ———. *Outlines of a Philosophy of the History of Man.* Trans-
        lated from German *Ideen zur Philosophie der Geschichte der
        Menschheit by T. Churchill.* New York: Berman Publishers,
        1966.
3:190   ———. *Reflections on the Philosophy of the History of Man-
        kind.* Abridged, and with an introduction by Frank E. Manuel.
        Chicago: University of Chicago Press, 1968.
3:191   Herr, Richard, and Harold T. Parker, eds. *Ideas in History:
        Essays Presented to Louis Gottschalk by his Former Students.*
        Durham, N.C.: Duke University Press, 1965.
3:192   Hexeter, J. H. *Doing History.* Bloomington: Indiana University
        Press, 1971.
3:193   ———. *The History Primer.* New York: Basic Books, 1971.
3:194   ———. *Reappraisals in History.* First ed., 4th impression.
        London: Longmans, 1967.
3:195   ———. "The Rhetoric of History," *History and Theory,* vol. 6,
        no. 1 (1967), pp. 3-13.
3:196   Higham, John. *History.* By John Higham, with Leonard Krieger
        and Felix Gilbert. Englewood Cliffs, N.J.: Prentice-Hall, 1965.
3:197   *History and the Concept of Time.* Middletown, Conn.: Wesleyan
        University Press, 1966.
3:198   History and Theory. *Studies in the Philosophy of History: Selected
        Essays from History and Theory.* By Carey B. Joynt and others.
        George H. Nadel, ed. New York: Harper & Row, 1965.
3:199   Hobart, Michael. "History and Religion in the Thought of Herbert

Butterfield," *Journal of the History of Ideas,* vol. 32, no. 4 (1971), pp. 543-554.

3:200 Hobsbawn, E. J. "From Social History to the History of Society," *Daedalus,* vol. 100, no. 2 (1971), pp. 20-45.

3:201 Hodgson, Peter Crafts. *The Formation of Historical Theology: A Study of Ferdinand Christian Baur.* New York: Harper & Row, 1966.

3:202 Hoffman, Ross John Swartz. *Tradition and Progress and other Historical Essays in Culture, Religion, and Politics.* Port Washington, N.Y.: Kennikat Press, 1968.

3:203 Hogeboom, Willard L. "The Cold War and Revisionist Historiography," *Social Studies,* vol. 61, no. 7 (1970), pp. 314-318.

3:204 Holborn, Hajo. *History and the Humanities.* Introduction by Leonard Krieger. 1st ed. Garden City, N.Y.: Doubleday, 1972.

3:205 ———. "The History of Ideas," *American Historical Review,* vol. 53, no. 3 (1968), pp. 683-695.

3:206 Hollinger, David A. "Perry Miller and Philosophical History," *History and Theory,* vol. 7, no. 2 (1968), pp. 189-202.

3:207 ———. "T. S. Kuhn's Theory of Science and Its Implications for History," *American Historical Review,* vol. 78, no. 2 (1973), pp. 370-393.

3:208 Horgan, Paul. "Journey to the Past and Return Reflections on the Work of the Historian," *Texas Quarterly,* vol. 13, no. 2 (1970), pp. 34-51.

3:209 Horkheimer, Max. "On the Concept of Freedom," *Diogenes,* vol. 53 (1966), pp. 73-81.

3:210 Hoyt, Nelly Noémie (Schargo). *History in the Encyclopedie.* New York: Octagon Books, 1970 [1947].

3:211 Hudson, Charles. "Folk History and Ethnohistory," *Ethnohistory,* vol. 13, no. 1-2 (1966), pp. 52-70.

3:212 Hughes, H. Stuart, ed. *Teachers of History: Essays in Honor of Lawrence Bradford Packard.* Freeport, N.Y.: Books for Libraries Press, 1970 [1954].

3:213 Humboldt, Wilhelm von. "On the Historian's Task," *History and Theory,* vol. 6, no. 1 (1967), pp. 57-71.

3:214 Ibn Khaldun. *The Muqaddimah: An Introduction to History.* Translated from Arabic by Franz Rosenthal. Abridged and edited by N. J. Dawood. Princeton, N.J.: Princeton University Press, 1969.

3:215 Iggers, Georg G. "The Idea of Progress: A Critical Reassessment," *American Historical Review*, vol. 71, no. 1 (1965), pp. 1-17.

3:216 Jackson, Barbara. *Nationalism and Ideology*. New York: Norton, 1966. Also, London: H. Hamilton, 1967.

3:217 Jackson, Gabriel. *Historian's Quest*. New York: Knopf, 1969.

3:218 James, Bernard. *The Death of Progress*. New York: Alfred A. Knopf, 1973.

3:219 Jarchow, Merrill E. "Exploring Local History, an Experience of Adventure, Anxiety, Exertion, and Success," *Minnesota History*, vol. 39, no. 7 (1965), pp. 265-271.

3:220 Johnson, Allen. *The Historian and Historical Evidence*. Port Washington, N.Y.: Kennikat Press, 1965 [1926].

3:221 Johnson, William M. "Syncretist Historians of Philosophy at Vienna," *Journal of the History of Ideas*, vol. 32, no. 2 (1971), pp. 299-305.

3:222 Jones, W. R. "Confronting World History," *Social Studies*, vol. 59, no. 7 (1968), pp. 328-337.

3:223 ———. "Western Historians and the World," *Indo-Asian Culture*, vol. 17, no. 2 (1968), pp. 6-11.

3:224 Jouvenel, Bertrand de. *The Art of Conjecture*. Translated by Nikita Lary. London: Weidenfeld and Nicolson, 1967.

3:225 Jovanovich, William. *Stations of Our Life*. New York: Harcourt, Brace & World, 1965.

3:226 Kahn, Sholom Jacob. *Science and Aesthetic Judgment: A Study in Taine's Critical Method*. Westport, Conn.: Greenwood Press, 1970 [1953].

3:227 Kármán, Mór. *A Brief Philosophy of History: Patterns of our Cultural Development*. Edited and with a foreword by August J. Molnar. New Brunswick, N.J.: American Hungarian Studies Foundation, 1972 [1908].

3:228 Keir, Sir David. "Old Ways and New in History," *Irish Historical Studies*, vol. 15, no. 59 (1967), pp. 214-227.

3:229 Keniston, Keith. "Accounting for Change," *Comparative Studies in Society and History*, vol. 7, no. 2 (1965), pp. 117-132.

3:230 Kennedy, D. E. "The Past and Present in Historical Writing," *Melbourne Historical Journal*, vol. 5 (1965), pp. 23-26.

3:231 Kennedy, P. M. "The Decline of Nationalistic History in the
West, 1900-1970," *Journal of Contemporary History*, vol. 8,
no. 1 (1973), pp. 77-100.

3:232 Kent, George O. "Clio the Tyrant: Historical Analogies and the
Meaning of History," *Historian*, vol. 32, no. 1 (1969), pp. 99-
106.

3:233 Keyes, Gordon Lincoln. *Christian Faith and the Interpretation
of History: A Study of St. Augustine's Philosophy of History.*
Lincoln: University of Nebraska Press, 1966.

3:234 Koenig, Duane. *Historians and History: Essays in Honor of
Charlton W. Tebeau.* Coral Gables, Fla.: University of Miami
Press, 1966.

3:235 Kolakowski, Leszek. *Marxism and Beyond: On Historical Under-
standing and Individual Responsibility.* Translated from the
Polish by Jane Zielonko Peel, introduction by Leopold Labedz.
London: Pall Mall, 1969.

3:236 Konrad, Nikolai Iosifovich. *West-East, Inseparable Twain:
Selected Articles.* Translated from Russian by H. Kasanina and
others. Moscow: Nauka Pub. House, Central Dept. of Oriental
Literature, 1967.

3:237 Kracauer, Siegfried. *History, the Last Thing Before the Last.*
New York: Oxford University Press, 1969.

3:238 ———. "Time and History," *History and Theory*, Beiheft 6
(1966), pp. 65-78.

3:239 Kramnick, Isaac. "Reflections on Revolution: Definitions and
Explanations in Recent Scholarship," *History and Theory*,
vol. 11, no. 1 (1972), pp. 26-63.

3:240 Krieger, Leonard. "Culture, Cataclysm, and Contingency,"
Journal of Modern History, vol. 40, no. 4 (1968), pp. 447-
473.

3:241 Krout, John A. "Some Thoughts on History Today," *New York
History*, vol. 49, no. 1 (1968), pp. 3-10.

3:242 Krug, Mark M. "History and the Social Sciences: The Narrowing
Gap," *Social Education*, vol. 29, no. 8 (1965), pp. 3-10.

3:243 ———. *History and the Social Sciences.* Waltham, Mass.:
Blaisdell, 1967.

3:244 Kuhn, Thomas S. *The Structure of Scientific Revolutions.* 2d ed.,
Chicago: University of Chicago Press, 1970.

3:245   Kuitert, Harminus Martinus. *The Reality of Faith: A Way Between Protestant Orthodoxy and Existentialist Theology.* Translated by Lewis B. Smedes. Grand Rapids, Mich.: W. B. Eerdmans Pub., 1968.

3:246   Kuklick, Bruce. "The Mind of the Historian," *History and Theory,* vol. 8, no. 3 (1969), pp. 313-331.

3:247   Kuzminski, Adrian. "The Problem of Historical Knowledge," *History and Theory,* vol. 12, no. 3 (1973), pp. 269-289.

3:248   Labriola, Antonio. *Essays on the Materialistic Conception of History.* Translated by Charles H. Kerr. New York: Monthly Review Press, 1966.

3:249   Lange, John. "The Arguments from Silence," *History and Theory,* vol. 5, no. 3 (1966), pp. 288-301.

3:250   Langmuir, Gavin I. "Tradition, History, and Prejudice," *Jewish Social Studies,* vol. 30, no. 3 (1968), pp. 147-168.

3:251   Laqueur, Walter Ze'ev, and George L. Mosse, eds. *The New History: Trends in Historical Research and Writing Since World War II.* By Karel Bartosek and others. New York: Harper & Row, 1967.

3:252   Lavrov, Petr Lavrovich. *Historical Letters.* Translated with an introduction and notes by James P. Scanlan. Berkeley: University of California Press, 1967.

3:253   Lawler, Justus G. "Circularity in History and Idea," *Clio,* vol. 2, no. 2 (1973), pp. 107-122.

3:254   Leff, Gordon. *History and Social Theory.* London: Merlin Press, 1969.

3:255   LeGoff, Jacques. "Is Politics Still the Backbone of History?," *Daedalus,* vol. 100, no. 2 (1971), pp. 1-19.

3:256   Lehmann, A. G. "The Writer as Canary," *Journal of Contemporary History,* vol. 2, no. 2 (1967), pp. 15-24.

3:257   Levine, Norman. "Humanism without Eschatology," *Journal of the History of Ideas,* vol. 33, no. 2 (1972), pp. 281-298.

3:258   Lewry, Osmund. *The Theology of History.* Notre Dame, Ind.: Fides Publishers, 1969.

3:259   Lewy, Guenther. "Historical Data in Comparative Politicial Analysis: A Note on Some Problems of Theory," *Comparative Politics,* vol. 1, no. 1 (1968), pp. 103-110.

3:260   Lichtheim, George. *The Concept of Ideology and other*

Essays. New York: Random House, 1967.

3:261	Liddel Hart, B. H. *Why Don't We Learn from History?* Rev. ed., New York: Hawthorn Books, 1971.

3:262	Liebel, Helen P. "The Historian and the Idea of World Civilization," *Dalhousie Review,* vol. 47, no. 4 (1968), pp. 455-466.

3:263	Lifton, Robert Jay. *History and Human Survival: Essays on the Young and Old Survivors and the Dead, Peace and War, and on Contemporary Psychohistory.* New York: Random House, 1970.

3:264	————. "Psychohistory," *Partisan Review,* vol. 37, no. 1 (1970), pp. 11-32.

3:265	————. "On Psychology and History," *Comparative Studies in Society and History,* vol. 7, no. 2 (1965), pp. 127-132.

3:266	Lindsay, George. *The Other History.* New York: Vantage Press, 1969.

3:267	Ling, J. F. "Explanation in History," *Mind,* vol. 75, no. 300 (1966), pp. 589-591.

3:268	Little, H. Ganse, Jr. "Ernst Troeltsch and the Scope of Historicism," *Journal of Religion,* vol. 46, no. 3 (1966), pp. 343-364.

3:269	————. "Ernst Troeltsch on History, Decision, and Responsibility." *Journal of Religion,* vol. 48, no. 3 (1968), pp. 205-234.

3:270	Loper, William Campbell. *The Lord of History.* Philadelphia: Westminster Press, 1965.

3:271	Lord, Clifford Lee, ed. *Keepers of the Past.* Chapel Hill: University of North Carolina Press, 1965.

3:272	Lottich, Kenneth V. "Arnold Toynbee and the Rhythm of History," *United Asia,* vol. 22, no. 1 (1970), pp. 41-43.

3:273	Louch, A. R. "History as Narrative," *History and Theory,* vol. 8, no. 1 (1969), pp. 54-70.

3:274	Louis, Wm. Roger, ed. *The Origins of the Second World War: A. J. P. Taylor and His Critics.* New York: John Wiley & Sons, 1972.

3:275	Löwith, Karl. *Nature, History, and Existentialism, and Other Essays in the Philosophy of History.* Edited with a critical introduction by Arnold Levison. Evanston, Ill.: Northwestern University Press, 1966.

3:276	————. *Permanence and Change: Lectures on the Philosophy of History.* Cape Town: Haum, 1969.

3:277 Lukacs, John A. *Historical Consciousness or the Remembered Past*. New York: Harper & Row, 1968.

3:278 Luthy, Herbert. "What's the Point of History?," *Journal of Contemporary History*, vol. 3, no. 2 (1968), pp. 3-22.

3:279 McCullagh, C. Behan. "Croce's Philosophy of History," *Historical Studies*, vol. 13, no. 49 (1967), pp. 86-93.

3:280 ———. "Historical Instrumentalism," *History and Theory*, vol. 12, no. 3 (1973), pp. 290-306.

3:281 ———. "Narrative and Explanation in History," *Mind*, vol. 78, no. 310 (1969), pp. 256-261.

3:282 Mandelbaum, Maurice. "A Theory of Justice," *History and Theory*, vol. 12, no. 2 (1973), pp. 240-250.

3:283 ———. *History, Man and Reason: A Study in Nineteenth-Century Thought*. Baltimore: Johns Hopkins Press, 1971.

3:284 Manuel, Frank E. *Freedom from History, and Other Untimely Essays*. New York: New York University Press, 1971.

3:285 ———. *Shapes of Philosophical History*. Stanford, Calif.: Stanford University Press, 1965.

3:286 ———. "The Use and Abuse of Psychology in History," *Daedalus*, vol. 100, no. 1 (1971), pp. 187-213.

3:287 Marc-Wogau, Konrad. *Philosophical Essays. History of Philosophy. Perception. Historical Explanation*. Edited by The Philosophical Society of Uppsala, Lund, Gleerup; Copenhagen: E. Monksgaard, 1967.

3:288 Marcus, John T. *Heaven, Hell and History: A Survey of Man's Faith in History from Antiquity to the Present*. New York: Macmillan, 1967.

3:289 Marías, Julián. *Generations: A Historical Method*. Translated by Harold C. Raley. University: University of Alabama Press, 1970.

3:290 Markus, Robert Austin. *Saeculum: History and Society in the Theology of St. Augustine*. Cambridge, Eng.: University Press, 1970.

3:291 Marrou, Henri Irénée. *The Meaning of History*. Translated by Robert J. Olsen. Baltimore: Helicon, 1966.

3:292 ———. *Time and Timeliness*. Translated by Violet Nevile. New York: Sheed and Ward, 1969.

3:293 Marshall, I. H. *Luke: Historian and Theologian*. Exeter: Paternoster Press, 1970 and Grand Rapids: Zondervan, 1971.

3:294 Martin, Charles G. *Christian Origins and History*. Harlow:
Longmans, 1969.

3:295 Martin, Rex. *Collingwood's Critique of the Concept of Human
Nature*. New York, 1967.

3:296 Marvin, Francis Sydney, ed. *The Evolution of World-Peace*.
Freeport, N.Y.: Books for Libraries Press, 1968.

3:297 Marwick, Arthur. *The Nature of History*. London: Macmillan,
1970, and New York: Alfred A. Knopf, 1971.

3:298 Marx, Karl. *Karl Marx on Colonialism and Modernization: His
Despatones and other Writings on China, India, Mexico, the
Middle East and North Africa*. Edited with introduction by
Shlomo Avineri. Garden City, N.Y.: Doubleday, 1968.

3:299 Mazlish, Bruce. "Group Psychology and Problems of Contemporary History," *Journal of Contemporary History*, vol.
3, no. 2 (1968), pp. 163-177.

3:300 ———. *The Riddle of History: The Great Speculators from
Vico to Freud*. New York: Harper & Row, 1966.

3:301 ———. "The Tragic Farce of Marx, Hegel and Engels: A Note,"
History and Theory, vol. 11, no. 3 (1972), pp. 335-337.

3:302 ———. "What is Psycho-History?," *Transactions of the Royal
Historical Society*, vol. 21 (1971), pp. 79-99.

3:303 Mead, Sidney E. "History and Identity," *Journal of Religion*,
vol. 51, no. 1 (1971), pp. 1-14.

3:304 Mieland, Jack W. "The Historical Relativism of Charles A.
Beard," *History and Theory*, vol. 12, no. 4 (1973), pp. 405-
413.

3:305 ———. *Scepticism and Historical Knowledge*. New York:
Random House, 1965.

3:306 Meinecke, Friedrich. *Historism: The Rise of a New Historical
Outlook: Translated from the German by J. E. Anderson*.
Translation revised by H. D. Schmidt; with a foreword by Sir
Isaiah Berlin. London: Routledge and Kegan Paul, 1972.

3:307 Millar, T. B. "On Writing About Foreign Policy," *Australian
Outlook*, vol. 21, no. 1 (1967), pp. 71-84.

3:308 *Milton and Clarendon: Two Papers on 17th Century English
Historiography*. Presented at a Seminar held at the Clark
Library on December 12, 1964, by French R. Fogle and
H. R. Trevor-Roper. Los Angeles: William Andrews Clark

Memorial Library. University of California, 1965.

3:309 *Mind, Science, and History.* Howard E. Kiefer and Milton E.
       Munitz, eds. Albany: State University of New York Press,
       1970.

3:310 Mink, Louis O. "The Autonomy of Historical Understanding,"
       History and Theory, vol. 5, no. 1 (1966), pp. 24-47.

3:311 ———. "Collingwood's Dialectic of History," *History and
       Theory,* vol. 7, no. 1 (1968), pp. 3-37.

3:312 ———. "Philosophical Analysis and Historical Understanding,"
       Review of Metaphysics, vol. 21, no. 4 (1968), pp. 667-698.

3:313 Mohan, Robert Paul. *Philosophy of History: An Introduction.*
       New York: Bruce Publishing, 1970.

3:314 Momigliano, Arnaldo. "Reconsidering B. Croce (1866-1952),"
       Durham University Journal, vol. 59, no. 1 (1966), pp. 1-21.

3:315 ———. *Studies in Historiography.* New York: Harper & Row,
       1966.

3:316 ———. "Tradition and the Classical Historian," *History and
       Theory,* vol. 11, no. 3 (1972), pp. 279-298.

3:317 ———. "Vico's Scienza Nuova: Roman 'Bestioni' and Roman
       'Eroi,'" *History and Theory,* vol. 5, no. 1 (1966), pp. 1-23.

3:318 Mommsen, Wolfgang. "Max Weber's Political Sociology and
       His Philosophy of World History," *International Social Science
       Journal,* vol. 17, no. 1 (1965), pp. 23-45.

3:319 Montgomery, John Warwick. *Where Is History Going? Essays in
       Support of the Historical Truth of the Christian Revolution.*
       With a commendatory letter by C. S. Lewis. Grand Rapids,
       Mich.: Zondervan Pub. House, 1969.

3:320 Moorehead, Alan. *A Late Education: Episodes in a Life.* London:
       Hamilton, 1970 and New York: Harper & Row, 1971.

3:321 Morely, John Morely, Viscount. *Notes on Politics and History:
       A University Address.* Port Washington, N.Y.: Kennikat Press,
       1971 [1914].

3:322 Morgan, George W. *The Human Predicament: Dissolution and
       Wholeness.* Providence: Brown University Press, 1968.

3:323 Müller, Gert. "History as a Rigorous Discipline," *History and
       Theory,* vol. 6, no. 3 (1967), pp. 299-312.

3:324 Mullett, Charles F. "The Dilemma of the Historian," *Social
       Education,* vol. 29, no. 6 (1965), pp. 345-348, 381.

58 HISTORIOGRAPHY AND PHILOSOPHY OF HISTORY

3:325 Munz, Peter. "The Skeleton and the Mollusc," *New Zealand Journal of History*, vol. 1, no. 2 (1967), pp. 107-123.
3:326 Murphey, Murray G. *Our Knowledge of the Historical Past.* Indianapolis: Bobbs-Merrill, 1973.
3:327 Murphy, George G. S. "On Counterfactual Propositions," *History and Theory*, beiheft 9 (1969), pp. 14-38.
3:328 ———. "Sir Isaiah Berlin on the Concept of Scientific History," *History and Theory*, vol. 4, no. 2 (1965), pp. 234-243.
3:329 ———. "The 'New' History," *Explorations in Entrepreneurial History*, vol. 2, no. 2 (1965), pp. 132-146.
3:330 Murray, Michael E. *Modern Philosophy of History: Its Origin and Destination.* The Hague: Martinus Nyhoff, 1970.
3:331 Nadel, George. "History as Psychology in Francis Bacon's Theory of History," *History and Theory*, vol. 5, no. 3 (1966), pp. 275-287.
3:332 Namier, Lewis Bernstein. *In the Margin of History.* Freeport, N.Y.: Books for Libraries Press, 1969.
3:333 Nash, Ronald H., ed. *Ideas of History.* New York: Dutton, 1969.
3:334 Navone, John J. *History and Faith in the Thought of Alan Richardson.* London: S. C. M. Press, 1966.
3:335 Nevins, Allan. *The Art of History; Two Lectures: The Old History and the New. Biography, History, and the Writing of Books.* By Catherine Drinker Bowen. Washington: Published for the Library of Congress by the Gertrude Clarke Whittall Poetry and Literature Fund, 1967.
3:336 Nevinson, Henry Wood. *In the Dark Backward.* Freeport, N.Y.: Books for Libraries Press, 1970.
3:337 Newman, John Henry. *Historical Sketches.* New ed., Westminster, M.D.: Christian Classics, 1970 [1872].
3:338 Nichols, Roy Franklin. *A Historian's Progress.* New York: Knopf, 1968.
3:339 ———. "History in a Self-Governing Culture," *American Historical Review*, vol. 72, no. 2 (1967), pp. 411-424.
3:340 Niebuhr, Reinhold. *Beyond Tragedy: Essays on the Christian Interpretation of History.* Freeport, N.Y.: Books for Libraries Press, 1971 [1937].
3:341 Nisbet, Robert A. *Social Change and History: Aspects of the*

Western Theory of Development. London, New York: Oxford
University Press, 1969.

3:342   ———. *Tradition and Revolt: Historical and Sociological Essays.*
New York: Random House, 1968.

3:343   ———. *The Social Philosophers: Community and Conflict in
Western Thought.* New York: Thomas Y. Crowell, 1973.

3:344   Norling, Bernard. *Timeless Problems in History.* Notre Dame:
University of Notre Dame Press, 1970.

3:345   Nota, Johannes Hille. *Phenomenology and History.* Translated
by Louis Grooten and the author. Chicago: Loyola University
Press, 1967.

3:346   Novack, George Edward. *Understanding History: Marxist Essays.*
New York: Pathfinder Press, 1972.

3:347   O'Brien, George Dennis. "Does Hegel Have a Philosophy of
History?," *History and Theory,* vol. 10, no. 3 (1971), pp.
195-317.

3:348   Ogden, H. V. S. "The Uses of History," *Michigan Quarterly
Review,* vol. 8, no. 1 (1969), pp. 21-26.

3:349   Ogletree, Thomas W. *Christian Faith and History: A Critical
Comparison of Ernst Troelisch and Karl Barth.* New York:
Abingdon Press, 1965.

3:350   Olafson, Frederick A. "Narrative History and the Concept of
Action," *History and Theory,* vol. 9, no. 3 (1970), pp. 265-
289.

3:351   O'Malley, Joseph J. "History and Man's 'Nature' in Marx,"
Review of Politics, vol. 28, no. 4 (1966), pp. 508-527.

3:352   Oman, Charles William Chadwick. *On the Writing of History.*
New York: Barnes & Noble, 1969 [1939].

3:353   Ortega y Gasset, José. *The Modern Theme.* New York: Harper
& Row, 1971 [1961].

3:354   Osborne, Arthur. *The Question of Progress.* Bombay: Bharatiya
Vidya Bhavan, 1966.

3:355   Paluch, Stanley. "The Specificity of Historical Language,"
History and Theory, vol. 7, no. 1 (1968), pp. 76-82.

3:356   Papaioannou, Kostas. "History and Theodicy," *Diogenes,* vol.
53 (1966), pp. 38-63.

3:357   Parkinson, G. H. R., ed. *Georg Lukacs: The Man, His Work and
His Ideas.* New York: Random House, 1970.

3:358   Partin, Robert. "The Use of History," *Alabama Review,* vol. 19, no. 2 (1966), pp. 109-124.

3:359   ———. "Voltaire's Historical Witticisms: A Case Study of Invalid Charges Against the Discipline," *Social Studies,* vol. 60, no. 6 (1969), pp. 261-263.

3:360   Patrides, C. A. *The Grand Design of God: The Literary Form of the Christian View of History.* London: Routledge and Kegan Paul, 1972.

3:361   *The Pattern of the Past: Can We Determine It?* Pieter Geyl, Arnold J. Toynbee and Pitirim A. Sorokin. New York: Greenwood Press, 1968 [1949].

3:362   Patterson, Lloyd George. *God and History in Early Christian Thought: A Study of Themes from Justin Martyr to Gregory the Great.* London: Black, 1967.

3:363   Peckham, Morse. "The Function of History in 19th-Century European Culture," *Survey,* vol. 17, no. 3 (1971), pp. 31-36.

3:364   Pelikan, Jaroslav. *The Finality of Jesus Christ in an Age of Universal History: A Dilemma of the Third Century.* Richmond: John Knox Press, 1965.

3:365   *Persecution and Liberty: Essays in Honor of George Lincoln Burr.* Freeport, N.Y.: Books for Libraries Press, 1968.

3:366   Peterson, Leland D. "Ezra Pound: The Use and Abuse of History," *American Quarterly,* vol. 17, no. 1 (1965), pp. 33-47.

3:367   *Physics, Logic and History: Based on the First International Colloquium Held at the University of Denver, May 16-20, 1966.* Contributors: Hermann Bondi and others. Wolfgang Yourgrau and Allen D. Breck, eds. New York: Plenum Press, 1970.

3:368   Pieper, Josef. *Hope and History.* Translated from German by Richard and Clara Winston. London: Burns & Oates, 1969.

3:369   Pierce, Donald John. *The Nature of History.* Ottawa, 1969.

3:370   Pius XI, Pope. *Essays in History, Written Between the Years 1896-1912, by Achille Ratt, now Pope Pius XI.* Freeport, N.Y.: Books for Libraries Press, 1967 [1934].

3:371   "The Place and Purpose of History," *Concordia Historical Institute Quarterly,* vol. 44, no. 2 (1971), pp. 51-56.

3:372   Plumb, John Harold. *The Death of the Past.* Boston: Houghton Mifflin, 1969 and London: Macmillan, 1969.

3:373   ———. "Gibbon and History," *History Today*, vol. 19, no. 11 (1969), pp. 737-743.

3:374   Pocock, John G. A. *Politics, Language and Time*. New York: Atheneum, 1971.

3:375   Pois, Robert A. "Two Poles Within Historicism: Croce and Meinecke," *Journal of the History of Ideas*, vol. 31, no. 2 (1970), pp. 253-272.

3:376   Pokora, Timoteus. "A Theory of Periodization of World History," *Archiv Orientalni*, vol. 34, no. 4 (1966), pp. 602-605.

3:377   Pollard, Sidney. *The Idea of Progress: History and Society*. New York: Basic Books, 1969.

3:378   Polos, Nicholas C. "Wooing the Muse Clio," *History Teacher*, vol. 5, no. 3 (1972), pp. 51-53.

3:379   Pompa, Leon. "Vico's Science," *History and Theory*, vol. 10, no. 1 (1969), pp. 49-83.

3:380   Popper, Karl R. *The Poverty of Historicism*. New York: Basic Books, 1967 [1960].

3:381   Porter, Daniel R. "Amateur and Professional History: An Observation," *Ohio History*, vol. 77, no. 4 (1968), pp. 145-148.

3:382   Post, John D. "Meteorological Historiography," *Journal of Interdisciplinary History*, vol. 3, no. 4 (1973), pp. 721-732.

3:383   Postan, M. M. "Fact and Relevance in Historical Study," *Historical Studies*, vol. 13, no. 51 (1968), pp. 411-425.

3:384   Pritzel, Konstantin. "A Critical Note on the Theory of Convergence," *Bulletin for the Institute of the Study of the U.S.S.R.*, vol. 18, no. 2 (1971), pp. 32-35.

3:385   Rabb, Thomas. "Guides to Quantitative History," *Historian*, vol. 35, no. 2 (1973), pp. 271-275.

3:386   Raghavachari, S. S. *The Unfolding Purpose*. Madras: University of Madras, 1969.

3:387   *Reappraisals: A New Look at History: The Social Sciences and History*. Walter Laqueur, George L. Mosse, eds. Jane Degras, Ernest Hearst, asst. eds. London: Weidenfeld and Nicolson, 1968.

3:388   Reeves, Marjorie. *The Figurae of Joachim of Fiore*. By Marjorie Reeves and Beatrice Hirsch-Reich. Oxford: Clarendon Press, 1972.

3:389 ————. *The Influence of Prophecy in the Later Middle Ages: A Study in Joachimism.* Oxford: Clarendon Press, 1969.

3:390 Regina, Sister Mary. "Las Casas: The Philosophy of His History," *Revista de Historia de América,* nos. 61-62 (1966), pp. 73-88.

3:391 *The Responsibility of Power: Historical Essays in Honor of Hajo Holborn.* Leonard Krieger and Fritz Stern, eds. London, Melbourne: Macmillan, 1968.

3:392 "Revisionism: A New Angry Look at the American Past," *Time,* vol. 95, no. 5 (1970), pp. 14-15.

3:393 Rhodes, James Ford. *Historical Essays.* Port Washington, N.Y.: Kennikat Press, 1966 [1909].

3:394 Richardson, Alan. *History: Sacred and Profane.* London: SCM Press, 1964.

3:395 Richardson, David Bonner. *Berdiaev's Philosophy of History. An Existentialist Theory of Social Creativity and Eschatology.* Preface by Charles Hartshorne. The Hague: Martinus Nijhoff, 1968.

3:396 Richter, Melvin, ed. *Essays in Theory and History: An Approach to the Social Sciences.* Cambridge, Mass.: Harvard University Press, 1970.

3:397 Riesterer, Berthold P. *Karl Löwith's View of History: A Critical Appraisal of Historicism.* The Hague: Martinus Nijhoff, 1969.

3:398 Roads, Christopher H. "Film as Historical Evidence," *Journal of the Society of Archivists,* vol. 3, no. 4 (1966), pp. 183-191.

3:399 Robinson, James Harvey. *The New History: Essays Illustrating the Modern Historical Outlook.* With a new introduction by Harvey Wish. New York: Free Press, 1965.

3:400 Robinson, James McConkey, and John B. Cobb, Jr., eds. *Theology as History.* New York: Harper & Row, 1967.

3:401 Rockwood, Raymond Oxley, ed. *Carl Becker's Heavenly City Revisited.* Hamden, Conn.: Archon Books, 1968 [1958].

3:402 Roller, Duane H. D., ed. *Perspectives in the History of Science and Technology.* Norman: University of Oklahoma Press, 1971.

3:403 Romulo, Carlos P. "The Responsibility of the Historian," *Pacific Historian,* vol. 11, no. 1 (1967), pp. 4-9.

3:404 Rosen, Lawrence. "Language, History and the Logic of Inquiry in Levi-Strauss and Sartre," *History and Theory,* vol. 10, no. 3 (1971), pp. 269-294.

3:405 Rotenstreich, Nathan. *Between Past and Present: An Essay on History.* Foreword by Martin Buber. Port Washington, N.Y.: Kennikat Press, 1973 [1958].

3:406 ———. "The Idea of Historical Progress and Its Assumptions," *History and Theory,* vol. 10, no. 2 (1971), pp. 197-227.

3:407 Rothman, Stanley. "Barrington Moore and the Dialectics of Revolution: An Essay Review," *American Political Science Review,* vol. 64, no. 1 (1970), pp. 61-82.

3:408 Rubinoff, Lionel. "Collingwood's Theory of the Relation Between Philosophy and History: A New Interpretation," *Journal of the History of Philosophy,* vol. 6, no. 4 (1968), pp. 363-380.

3:409 Rutman, Darret B. "Notes to the Underground: Historiography," *Journal of Interdisciplinary History,* vol. 3, no. 2 (1972), pp. 373-383.

3:410 Salvemini, Gaetano. *Historian and Scientist: An Essay on the Nature of History and the Social Sciences.* Freeport, N.Y.: Books for Libraries Press, 1969 [1939].

3:411 Sanders, Jennings Bryan. *Historical Interpretations and American Historianship.* Yellow Springs, Ohio: Antioch Press, 1966.

3:412 Savelle, Max. *Is Liberalism Dead? And Other Essays.* Seattle: University of Washington Press, 1967.

3:413 Schlegel, Friedrich von. *The Philosophy of History. In a Course of Lectures, Delivered at Vienna.* Translated from German, with a Memoir of the author by James Burton Robinson. 7th ed., revised. London: G. Bell, 1883. St. Clair Shores, Mich.: Scholarly Press, 1970.

3:414 Schlesinger, Arthur J. "The Historian as Participant," *Daedalus,* vol. 100, no. 2 (1971), pp. 323-339.

3:415 Schlesinger, Arthur M., Jr. "On the Inscrutability of History," *Encounter,* vol. 27, no. 158 (1966), pp. 10-17.

3:416 ———. "Nationalism and History," *Journal of Negro History,* vol. 54, no. 1 (1969), pp. 19-31.

3:417 Schmitt, Bernadotte Everly, ed. *Some Historians of Modern Europe: Essays in Historiography.* Port Washington, N.Y.: Kennikat Press, 1966 [1942].

3:418 Schouler, James. *Historical Briefs.* Freeport, N.Y.: Books for Libraries Press, 1972 [1806].

3:419 Schu, Pierre. *The World of Great Men: History Told Through*

the Lives of the Men Who Made It. Illustrated by Dorothy
Koch. North Easton, Mass.: Holy Cross Press, 1967.

3:420   Scudder, John R., Jr. and Barbara Gulick. "History's Purpose:
Becker or Ortega?," *History Teacher,* vol. 5, no. 4 (1972),
pp. 41-45.

3:421   Sée, Henri Eugène. *The Economic Interpretation of History.*
Translation and introduction by Melvin M. Knight. New York:
A. M. Kelley, 1968.

3:422   Sewell, William. "Marc Bloch and the Logic of Comparative
History," *History and Theory,* vol. 6, no. 2 (1967), pp. 208-
218.

3:423   Shankel, George Edgar. *God and Man in History: A Study in
the Christian Understanding of History.* Nashville: Southern
Pub. Association, 1967.

3:424   Sharma, B. M. and L. P. Choundhry. *Expanding Dimensions of
Freedom.* Agra: Oriental Pub. House, 1967.

3:425   Sharrock, Roger. *Carlyle and the Sense of History.* London:
1966.

3:426   Shiner, Larry. "A Phenomenological Approach to Historical
Knowledge," *History and Theory,* vol. 8, no. 3 (1969), pp.
260-274.

3:427   Simon, H. Paul. "The 'Fox' Versus the 'Hedgehog.'" *Queen's
Quarterly,* vol. 78, no. 1 (1971), pp. 40-53.

3:428   Sinclair, Keith. "On Writing Shist," *Historical Studies,* vol. 13,
no. 51 (1968), pp. 426-432.

3:429   Sivashankar, N. *Man Rediscovered: A New Approach to the
Nature of Man: An Attempt at a Synthesis of Ancient
Philosophies of Religions and Modern Philosophies of Science.*
Trivandrum: B. Sarada Amma, 1965.

3:430   Skinner, Andrew. "Natural History in the Age of Adam Smith,"
Political Studies, vol. 15, no. 1 (1967), pp. 32-48.

3:431   Skinner, Quentin. "The Limits of Historical Explanations,"
Philosophy, vol. 41, no. 157 (1966), pp. 199-215.

3:432   ———. "Meaning and Understanding in the History of Ideas,"
History and Theory, vol. 8, no. 1 (1969), pp. 3-53.

3:433   Skotheim, Robert Allen, ed. *The Historian and the Climate of
Opinion.* Reading, Mass.: Addison-Wesley Pub., 1969.

3:434   Smith, Goldwin. *Lectures on Modern History, Delivered in Oxford, 1859-61.* Freeport, N.Y.: Books for Libraries Press, 1972 [1861].

3:435   Smith, John E. "Time, Times, and the 'Right Time?,' Chronos and Kairos," *Monist,* LIII (Jan. 1969), 1 ff.

3:436   Smith, Ronald Gregor. *Secular Christianity.* London: Collins, 1966.

3:437   Somervell, David Churchill. *Studies in Statesmanship.* Port Washington, N.Y.: Kennikat Press, 1970.

3:438   Spitzer, Alan B. "The Historical Problem of Generations," *American Historical Review,* vol. 78, no. 5 (1973), pp. 1353-1386.

3:439   Sprinzak, Ehud. "Thesis as an Historical Explanation," *History and Theory,* vol. 11, no. 3 (1972), pp. 294-320.

3:440   Stalnaker, Robert. "Events, Periods, and Institutions in Historians' Language," *History and Theory,* vol. 6, no. 2 (1967), pp. 159-179.

3:441   Starn, Randolph. "Historians and Crisis," *Past and Present,* no. 52 (1971), pp. 3-22.

3:442   Starr, Chester. "Historical and Philosophical Time," *History and Theory,* beiheft 6 (1967), pp. 24-35.

3:443   Stearns, Peter N. "Some Comment on Social History," *Journal of Social History,* vol. 1, no. 1 (1967), pp. 3-6.

3:444   Stern, Fritz Richard, ed. *The Varieties of History: From Voltaire to the Present.* 2nd ed. London: Macmillan, 1970.

3:445   Stegner, Wallace. "On the Writing of History," *American West,* vol. 2, no. 4 (1965), pp. 6-13.

3:446   Steuwer, Rodger H. *Historical and Philosophical Perspectives of Science.* Minneapolis, 1970.

3:447   Stevenson, W. Taylor. *History as Myth: The Import for Contemporary Theology.* New York: Seabury Press, 1969.

3:448   Stinnette, Charles R., Jr. "Insight, History and Religion," *Christian Scholar,* vol. 49, no. 3 (1966), pp. 177-183.

3:449   Stocking, George W. Race. *Culture and Revolution.* New York: Free Press, 1968.

3:450   Stover, Robert Capner. *The Nature of Historical Thinking.* Chapel Hill: University of North Carolina Press, 1967.

3:451   ———. "Responsibility for the Cold War—A Case Study in
        Historical Responsibility," *History and Theory,* vol. 11, no. 2
        (1972), pp. 145-178.
3:452   Strong, Tracy B. "History and Choices: The Foundations of
        the Political Thought of Raymond Aron," *History and Theory,*
        vol. 11, no. 2 (1972), pp. 179-192.
3:453   Strout, Cushing. "Ego Psychology and the Historian," *History
        and Theory,* vol. 7, no. 3 (1968), pp. 281-297.
3:454   ———. "Review Essay of Richard Hofstadter *The Progressive
        Historians* (New York: Alfred A. Knopf, 1968)," *History and
        Theory,* vol. 9, no. 2 (1970), pp. 230-236.
3:455   Sturley, D. M. *The Study of History.* Harlow: Longmans, 1969.
3:456   Sturtevant, William C. "Anthropology, History and Ethnohistory,"
        Ethnohistory, vol. 13, no. 1-2 (1966), pp. 1-51.
3:457   Sullivan, John Edward. *Prophets of the West: An Introduction
        to the Philosophy of History.* New York: Holt, Rinehart, and
        Winston, 1970.
3:458   Sutherland, Lucy Stuart. *Studies in History: British Academy
        Lectures by Z. N. Brooke and others.* London, New York:
        Oxford University Press, 1966.
3:459   Sweet, Paul R. "Wilhelm von Humboldt (1767-1835): His
        Legacy to the Historian," *Centennial Review,* vol. 15, no. 1
        (1971), pp. 23-37.
3:460   Szasz, Ferenc. "The Meaning of History," *Historian,* vol. 30,
        no. 2 (1968), pp. 238-243.
3:461   Tapp, E. J. *Man and His History.* Armidale, N.S.W.: University
        of New England, 1971.
3:462   Tarlton, Charles D. "Historicity, Meaning and Revisionism in
        the Study of Political Thought," *History and Theory,* vol. 12,
        no. 3 (1973), pp. 307-328.
3:463   Taylor, Alan John Percivale. *Politics in Wartime, and Other
        Essays.* New York: Atheneum, 1965.
3:464   Taylor, Donald S. "R. G. Collingwood: Art, Craft and History,"
        Clio, vol. 2, no. 3 (1973), pp. 239-280.
3:465   Taylor, Edmond. *Awakening from History.* Boston: Gambit,
        1969.
3:466   Taylor, Henry Osborn. *A Historian's Creed.* Port Washington,
        N.Y.: Kennikat Press, 1969 [1939].

3:467 Thernstrom, Stephan. "Notes on the Historical Study of Mobility," *Comparative Studies in Society and History,* vol. 10, no. 2 (1968), pp. 162-172.

3:468 Thompson, James Westfall, and Bernard J. Holm. *A History of Historical Writing.* 2 vols. Gloucester, Mass.: Peter Smith, 1967 [1942].

3:469 Thomson, David. *The Aims of History: Values of the Historical Attitude.* London: Thames & Hudson, 1969.

3:470 ————. "Must History Stay Nationalist? A Prison of Closed Intellectual Frontiers," *Encounter,* vol. 30, no. 177 (1968), pp. 22-28.

3:471 Thorne, Christopher G. *Ideology and Power: Studies in Major Ideas and Events of the Twentieth Century.* London: Collier-Macmillan; New York: Macmillan, 1965.

3:472 Tillinghast, Pardon E. *The Specious Past: Historians and Others.* Reading, Mass.: Addison-Wesley Pub. Co., 1972.

3:473 Tocqueville, Alexis de. "Characteristics of Historians in Democratic Times," *Journal of Historical Studies,* vol. 1, no. 2 (1967), pp. 20-23.

3:474 Todd, William Lewis. *History as Applied Science: A Philosophical Study.* Detroit: Wayne State University Press, 1972.

3:475 Topolski, Jerzy. "Levi-Strauss and Marx on History," *History and Theory,* vol. 12, no. 2 (1973), pp. 192-207.

3:476 Toulmin, Stephen. "Rediscovering History: New Directions in the Philosophy of Science," *Encounter,* vol. 36, no. 1 (1971), pp. 53-64.

3:477 Toynbee, Arnold Joseph. *Experiences.* London, New York: Oxford University Press, 1969.

3:478 ————. *A Study of History.* Abridgement of volumes by D. C. Somervell. New York: Dell Pub., 1965 [1946], and London: Oxford University Press, 1972.

3:479 Trevelyan, George Macaulay. *Clio, A Muse and Other Essays.* Freeport, N.Y.: Books for Libraries Press, 1968.

3:480 Trevor-Roper, Hugh Redwald. "Historical Knowledge," *Survey,* vol. 17, no. 3 (1971), pp. 2-12.

3:481 ————. *The Past and the Present: History and Sociology: Oration Delivered at the London School of Economics and Political Science on Thursday, December 5, 1968, by H. R.*

Trevor-Roper. London: London School of Economics and
Political Science, 1969.
3:482   Trotter, F., ed. *Jesus and the Historian.* Festschrift for E. C.
Colwell. Philadelphia: Westminster Press, 1968.
3:483   Trueman, John Herbert. *The Anatomy of History.* Toronto:
J. M. Dent, 1967.
3:484   Tuttle, Howard Nelson. *Wilhelm Dilthey's Philosophy of Historical Understanding: A Critical Analysis.* Leiden: E. J. Brill,
1969.
3:485   Unger, Rudolf. "The Problem of Historical Objectivity: A
Sketch of Its Development Since the Time of Hegel," *History
and Theory,* vol. 10, Beiheft 11 (1971), pp. 60-86.
3:486   *The Uses of History: Essays in Intellectual and Social History.
Presented to William J. Bossenbrook.* Compiled and edited by
Hayden V. White, with a foreword by Alfred H. Kelly.
Detroit: Wayne State University Press, 1968.
3:487   Villari, Pasquale. *Studies, Historical and Critical.* Translated by
Linda Villari. Freeport, N.Y.: Books for Libraries, 1968
[1907].
3:488   Viner, Jacob. *The Role of Providence in the Social Order: An
Essay in Intellectual History.* Memoirs of the American
Philosophical Society, volume 90. Jayne Lectures for 1966.
Philadelphia: the Society, 1972.
3:489   Voltaire, François Marie Arouet de. *The Philosophy of History.*
With a preface by Thomas Kiernan. New York: Philosophical
Library, 1965 [1766].
3:490   Von Laue, T. H. "Is There a Crisis in the Writing of History?,"
Bucknell Review, vol. 14, no. 3 (1966), pp. 1-15.
3:491   Von Mises, Ludwig. *Theory and History: An Interpretation of
Social and Economic Evolution.* New Rochelle, N.Y.: Arling-
ton House, 1969.
3:492   Von Ranke, Leopold. *The Theory and Practice of History.*
Edited with an introduction by Georg G. Iggers and Konrad
von Moltke. Indianapolis: Bobbs-Merrill, 1973 [1901].
3:493   Von Schiller, Friedrich. "The Nature and Value of Universal
History: An Inaugural Lecture [1789]," *History and Theory,*
vol. 11, no. 3 (1972), pp. 321-334.
3:494   Walsh, William Henry. *An Introduction to Philosophy of History.*
3rd revised edition. London: Hutchinson, 1967.

3:495 Wand, John William Charles, Bp. of London. *Christianity: A Historical Religion.* Valley Forge, Pa.: Judson Press, 1972.

3:496 Wang, Gungwu. *The Use of History.* Athens: Ohio University, Center for International Studies, 1968.

3:497 Ward, Russel Braddock. *Uses of History.* Armidale, N.S.W.: University of New England, 1968.

3:498 Wasiolek, Edward. "The Theory of History in War and Peace," *Midway,* vol. 9, no. 2 (1968), pp. 117-135.

3:499 Watt, Donald C. "Contemporary History: Problems and Perspectives," *History and Theory,* vol. 7, no. 1 (1968), pp. 38-59.

3:500 Weingartner, Rudolph. "Philosophic Comments on Cultural History," *History and Theory,* vol. 7, no. 1 (1968), pp. 38-59.

3:501 Weinstein, Fred and Gerald M. Platt. "History and Theory: The Question of Psychoanalysis," *Journal of Interdisciplinary History,* vol. 4 (1972), pp. 419-434.

3:502 Weintraub, Karl Joachim. *Visions of Culture.* Chicago: University of Chicago Press, 1966.

3:503 Westcott, Roger W. "The Enumeration of Civilizations," *History and Theory,* vol. 9, no. 1 (1970), pp. 59-85.

3:504 Whalley, Peter. *An Essay on the Manner of Writing History.* New York: Garland Pub., 1970.

3:505 White, Hayden V. "Croce and Becker: A Note on the Evidence of Influence," *History and Theory,* vol. 10, no. 2 (1971), pp. 222-227.

3:506 ———. "The Politics of Contemporary Philosophy of History," *Clio,* vol. 3, no. 1 (1973), pp. 35-53.

3:507 ———. "The Tasks of Intellectual History," *Monist,* vol. 53, no. (1969), pp. 619-

3:508 White, Morton Gabriel. *Foundations of Historical Knowledge.* New York: Harper & Row, 1965.

3:509 Widgery, Alban Gregory. *The Meanings in History.* London: Allen & Unwin, 1967.

3:510 Wilburn, Ralph Glenn. *The Historical Shape of Faith.* Philadelphia: Westminster Press, 1966.

3:511 Wilde, Oscar. *The Rise of Historical Criticism.* Folcroft, Pa.: Folcroft Press, 1969 [1905].

3:512 Wilkins, Burleigh. "Teleology in Kant's Philosophy of History,"

History and Theory, vol. 5, no. 2 (1966), pp. 172-185.

3:513 Wilson, Edmund. *To the Finland Station: A Study in the Writing and Acting of History.* With a new introduction. New York: Farrar, Straus and Giroux, 1972.

3:514 Winkler, Fred H. "Some Suggested Laws of Diplomatic History," *Social Studies,* vol. 58, no. 3 (1967), pp. 114-120.

3:515 Witschi-Bernz, Astrid. "Main Trends in Historical Method Literature: Sixteenth to Eighteenth Centuries," *History and Theory,* Beiheft 12 (1972), pp. 50-90.

3:516 Wolfson, Harry Austryn. *Studies in the History of Philosophy and Religion.* Vol. 1, ed. by Isadore Twersky and George H. Williams. Cambridge, Mass.: Harvard University Press, 1973.

3:517 Wolman, Benjamin B., ed. *The Psychoanalytic Interpretation of History.* Foreword by William L. Langer. New York: Basic Books, 1971.

3:518 Woodbridge, Frederick James Eugene. *The Purpose of History.* Port Washington, N.Y.: Kennikat Press, 1965 [1916].

3:519 Woodward, Comer Vann. *The Age of Reinterpretation.* Washington: Service Center for Teachers of History, 1968 [1961].

3:520 ———. "History and the Third Culture," *Journal of Contemporary History,* vol. 3, no. 2 (1968), pp. 23-35.

3:521 Wroblewski, Sergius. *A Prophetic History of the West.* Staten Island, N.Y.: Alba House, 1968.

3:522 Wurgait, Lewis D. *Bibliography of Works in the Philosophy of History, 1962-1965.* Bibliography of signed works by Elie Halevy, compiled by Melvin Richter. Middletown, Conn.: Wesleyan University Press, 1969.

3:523 Wylie, Kenneth C. "The Uses and Misuses of Ethnohistory," *Journal of Interdisciplinary History,* vol. 3, no. 4 (1973), pp. 707-720.

3:524 Young, Louise (Merwin). *Thomas Carlyle and the Art of History.* New York: Octagon Books, 1971 [1939].

3:525 Young, Norman James. *History and Existential Theology: The Role of History in the Thought of Rudolf Bultmann.* Philadelphia: Westminster Press, 1969.

3:526 Zinn, Howard. *The Politics of History.* Boston: Beacon Press, 1970.

4. HISTORIOGRAPHICAL STUDIES BY AREA AND DISCIPLINE

AFRICA

4:1 Ayandele, E. A. "How Truly Nigerian Is Our Nigerian History?," *African Notes*, vol. 5, no. 2 (1969), pp. 19-35.

4:2 Brooks, George E. "A Schema for Integrating Africa Into World History," *History Teacher*, vol. 3, no. 2 (1970), pp. 5-19.

4:3 Gordon, David C. *Self-determination and History in the Third World.* Princeton, N.J.: Princeton University Press, 1971.

4:4 Hooker, James R. "African History in General Education: Can Africans Rejoin World History?," *Journal of Human Relations*, vol. 15, no. 1 (1967), pp. 44-52.

4:5 Jones, D. H. "Problems of African Chronology," *Journal of African History*, vol. 11, no. 2 (1970), pp. 161-176.

4:6 McCall, Daniel F. *Africa in Time Perspective. A Discussion of Historical Reconstruction from Unwritten Sources.* New York: Oxford University Press, 1969.

4:7 Marks, Shula. "African and Afrikaner History," *Journal of African History*, vol. 11, no. 3 (1970), pp. 435-447.

4:8 Tignor, Robert L. "African History and the Social Studies," *Journal of Modern African Studies*, vol. 4, no. 3 (1966), pp. 349-357.

4:9 Wansborough, John. "The Decolonization of North African History," *Journal of African History*, vol. 9, no. 4 (1968), pp. 643-650.

ANCIENT AND CLASSICAL HISTORY

4:10 Austin, Norman. *The Greek Historians: Herodotus, Thucydides, Polybius, Plutarch; Introduction and Selected Readings.* New York: Van Nostrand-Reinhold, 1969.

4:11 Bridenthal, Renate. "Was There a Roman Homer? Niebuhr's Thesis and Its Critics," *History and Theory*, vol. 11, no. 2 (1972), pp. 193-213.

4:12 Bruce, I. A. F. "Theopompus and Classical Greek Historiography," *History and Theory*, vol. 9, no. 1 (1970), pp. 86-109.

4:13 Den-Boer, W. "Graeco-Roman Historiography in its Relation to
      Biblical and Modern Thinking," *History and Theory,* vol. 9,
      no. 1 (1968), pp. 60-75.
4:14 Finley, M. I. "Myth, Memory, and History," *History and Theory,*
      vol. 4, no. 3 (1965), pp. 281-302.
4:15 Grant, Michael. *The Ancient Historians.* New York: Charles
      Scribner's Sons, 1970.
4:16 Katz, Solomon. "Remembrance of Things Past," *Pacific Historical
      Review,* vol. 38, no. 1 (1969), pp. 1-20.
4:17 Lapp, Paul W. *Biblical Archaeology and History.* New York:
      World, 1969.
4:18 Millward, G. E., G. W. Evans and L. E. Hull. "Atlantis: Modern
      Theories and Ancient Tales," *History Today,* vol. 23 (July
      1973), pp. 503-506.
4:19 Momigliano, Arnaldo. "Time in Ancient Historiography," *History
      and Theory,* Beiheft 6 (1966), pp. 1-23.
4:20 Padden, R. C. "On Diffusionism and Historicity," *American
      Historical Review,* vol. 78, no. 4 (1973), pp. 987-1004.

ASIA

4:21 Chesneaux, Jean. "For an Asian History of Modern Asia,"
      Diogenes, vol. 51 (1966), pp. 104-119.
4:22 Evans, Hubert. "Fifty Years of Soviet Oriental and African
      Historical Study," *Central Asian Review,* vol. 16, no. 4 (1968),
      pp. 294-298.
4:23 ———. "Recent Soviet Writing on Afghanistan," *Central Asian
      Review,* vol. 15, no. 4 (1967), pp. 294-298.
4:24 Gabrieli, Frencesco. "Apology for Orientalism," *Diogenes,* vol.
      50 (1965), pp. 128-136.
4:25 Hanks, Lucien M. "Bang Chan and Bangkok: Five Perspectives on
      the Relation of Local to National History," *Journal of South-
      east Asian History,* vol. 8, no. 2 (1967), pp. 250-256.
4:26 Jansen, Marius B. "American Studies in Japan," *American
      Historical Review,* vol. 7, no. 2 (1965), pp. 413-417.
4:27 Larkin, John A. "The Place of Local History in Philippine
      Historiography," *Journal of Southeast Asian History,* vol. 8,
      no. 2 (1967), pp. 306-317.

4:28 *Recent Trends in Japanese Historiography: Bibliographical Essays; Japan at the XIIIth International Congress of Historical Sciences in Moscow.* Edited by the Japanese National Committee of Historical Sciences. Tokyo, Japan: Society for the Promotion of Science, 1970.

4:29 Thornton, Richard C. "Soviet Historians and China's Past," *Problems of Communism,* vol. 17, no. 2 (1968), pp. 71-75.

3:30 Wang, Gungwu. "Malaysia's Social History," *Peninjau Sejarah,* vol. 1, no. 2 (1966), pp. 1-5.

4:31 Webb, Herschel. *Research in Japanese Sources: A Guide.* New York: Columbia University Press, 1965.

4:32 Wheeler, Geoffrey. "A New Look at Oriental Studies," *Journal of the Royal Central Asian Society,* vol. 55, no. 1 (1968), pp. 12-19.

4:33 Wittfogel, Karl A. "Results and Problems of the Study of Oriental Despotism," *Journal of Asian Studies,* vol. 28, no. 2 (1969), pp. 357-365.

4:34 Wright, Arthur F., and John W. Hall. "Chinese and Japanese Historiography; Some Trends, 1961-1966," *Annals of the American Academy of Political and Social Science,* vol. 371 (1967), pp. 178-193.

4:35 Yi Hong-jik. "Tasks for Korean Studies: History," *Asiatic Research Bulletin,* vol. 8, no. 4 (1965), pp. 1-5.

AUSTRALIA

4:36 Young, J. D. "South Australian Historians and Wakefield's 'Scheme,'" *Historical Studies,* vol. 14, no. 53 (1969), pp. 32-53.

AUSTRIA

4:37 Sweet, Paul R. "Historical Writing of Heinrich von Srbik," *History and Theory,* vol. 9, no. 1 (1970), pp. 37-58.

BRAZIL

4:38 Bartley, Russell H. "A Decade of Soviet Scholarship in Brazilian History: 1958-1968," *Hispanic American Historical*

Review, vol. 50, no. 3 (1970), pp. 445-466.

4:39   Burns, E. Bradford. *Perspectives in Brazilian History.* New York:
       Columbia University Press, 1967.

4:40   Conrad, Robert. "Joâo Capistrano de Abreu, Brazilian Historian,"
       Revista de Historia de América, no. 59 (1965), pp. 149-164.

4:41   Schwartz, Stuart B. "Francisco Adolfo de Varnhagen: Diplomat,
       Patriot, Historian," *Hispanic American Historical Review,* vol.
       47, no. 2 (1967), pp. 184-202.

BUSINESS HISTORY

4:42   Baugham, James P. "Recent Trends in the Business History of
       Latin America," *Business History Review,* vol. 39, no. 4 (1965),
       pp. 425-438.

4:43   Cole, Arthur H. "Aggregative Business History," *Business History
       Review,* vol. 39, no. 3 (1965), pp. 287-300.

4:44   Herlihy, David. "Raymond de Rooven: Historian of Mercantile
       Capitalism," *Journal of European Economic History,* vol. 1
       (Winter 1972), pp. 755-762.

CANADA

4:45   Careless, J. M. S. "The *Review* Reviewed: Or Fifty Years With
       the Beaver Patrol," *Canadian Historical Review,* vol. 51, no. 1
       (1970), pp. 48-70.

4:46   Ogelsby, John C. M. "Latin American Studies in Canada," *Latin
       American Research Review,* vol. 1, no. 2 (1966), pp. 80-88.

CHURCH HISTORY

4:47   Outler, Albert C. "Theodosius' Horse: Reflections on the Predica-
       ment of the Church Historian," *Church History,* vol. 34, no. 3
       (1965), pp. 251-261.

CULTURAL HISTORY

4:48   Jones, Howard Mumford. "The Nature of Literary History,"
       Journal of the History of Ideas, vol. 28, no. 2 (1967), pp.
       147-160.

CZECHOSLOVAKIA

4:49   Balik, Stanislav. "Anglo-American History of Law Until 1918: Its
Teaching and Research at the Law Faculty of the Charles Uni-
versity in Prague, Czechoslovakia," *American Journal of Legal
History,* vol. 10, no. 2 (1966), pp. 178-181.

4:50   Bartosek, Karel. "Czechoslovakia: The State of Historiography,"
Journal of Contemporary History, vol. 2, no. 1 (1967), pp.
143-155.

4:51   Winters, Stanley B. "Trends in Labor Historiography in Czechoslovakia," *Labor History,* vol. 10, no. 4 (1969), pp. 602-629.

EASTERN EUROPE

4:52   Pech, Stanley Z. "New Avenues in Eastern European History,"
Canadian Slavonic Papers, vol. 10, no. 1 (1968), pp. 3-18.

ECONOMIC HISTORY

4:53   Bergier, Jean-François. "New Tendencies in Economic History,"
Diogenes, vol. 58 (1967), pp. 104-122.

4:54   Hughes, J. R. T. "Fact and Theory in Economic History,"
Explorations in Entrepreneurial History, vol. 3, no. 2 (1966),
pp. 75-100.

4:55   Hunt, E. H. "The New Economic History: Professor Fogel's
Study of American Railways," *History,* vol. 53, no. 177 (1968),
pp. 3-18.

4:56   Redlich, Fritz. " 'New' and Traditional Approaches to Economic
History and Their Interdependence," *Journal of Economic
History,* vol. 25, no. 4 (1965), pp. 480-496.

4:57   Schweitzer, Arthur. "Economic Systems and Economic History,"
Journal of Economic History, vol. 25, no. 4 (1965), pp. 660-
679.

EUROPE

4:58   *Anniversary Essays in Mediaeval History by Students of Charles
Homer Haskins, Presented on his Completion of Forty Years
of Teaching.* Freeport, N.Y.: Books for Libraries Press, 1967.

4:59   Burke, Peter. *The Renaissance Sense of the Past.* London: Edward

Arnold, 1969, and New York: St. Martin's Press, 1970.

4:60   Cantor, Norman F. *Perspectives on the European Past: Conversations with Historians.* New York: Macmillan, 1971.

4:61   Cate, James Lea, and Eugene N. Anderson. *Medieval and Historiographical Essays in Honor of James Westfall Thompson.* Port Washington, N.Y.: Kennikat Press, 1966 [1938].

4:62   *Contemporary History in Europe.* Donald Cameron Watt, ed., under the auspices of the Institute of Contemporary History and Wiener Library, London. Introduction by Alan Bullock. London: Allen & Unwin, 1969.

4:63   *The Crusades, and Other Historical Essays; Presented to Dana O. Munro by His Former Students.* Edited by Louis J. Paetow. Freeport, N.Y.: Books for Libraries Press, 1968 [1928].

4:64   *Essays in Intellectual History, Dedicated to James Harvey Robinson by His Former Seminar Students.* Freeport, N.Y.: Books for Libraries Press, 1968 [1929].

4:65   Halperin, S. William, ed. *Essays in Modern European Historiography.* Chicago: University of Chicago Press, 1970.

4:66   Mendels, Franklin. "Recent Research in European Historical Demography," *American Historical Review,* vol. 75, no. 4 (1970), pp. 1065-1073.

4:67   Oakley, Francis. "Celestial Hierarchies Revisited: Walter Ullman's Vision of Medieval Politics," *Past and Present,* no. 60 (1973), pp. 3-48.

4:68   Schmitt, Bernadotte E., ed. *Some Historians of Modern Europe.* Port Washington, N.Y.: Kennikat Press, 1966 [1942].

4:69   Schmitt, Hans A., ed. *Historians of Modern Europe.* Baton Rouge: Louisiana State University Press, 1971.

4:70   Stubbs, William. *Seventeen Lectures on the Study of Medieval and Modern History and Kindred Subjects, Delivered at Oxford, Under Statutory Obligation in the Years 1867-1884.* New York: H. Fertig, 1967.

4:71   Trevor-Roper, Hugh Redwald. *The Romantic Movement and the Study of History; the John Coffin Memorial Lecture Delivered Before the University of London on February 17, 1969.* London: Athlone Press, 1969.

FRANCE

4:72   Ben-Israel, Hedva. *English Historians on the French Revolu-*

tion. London: Cambridge University Press, 1968.
4:73   Cobban, Alfred. "Hippolyte Taine, Historian of the French
       Revolution," *History,* vol. 53, no. 179 (1968), pp. 331-341.
4:74   Geismar, Peter. "Latin American Studies in France," *Latin Ameri-
       can Research Review,* vol. 3, no. 4 (Fall 1968), pp. 45-51.
4:75   Goubert, Pierre. "Historical Demography and the Reinterpreta-
       tion of Early Modern French History: A Research Review,"
       Journal of Interdisciplinary History, vol. 1, no. 1 (1970), pp.
       37-48.
4:76   Huppert, George. *The Idea of Perfect History: Historical Erudi-
       tion and Historical Philosophy in France.* Urbana: University
       of Illinois Press, 1970.
4:77   Kelley, Donald R. *Foundations of Modern Historical Scholar-
       ship: Language, Law and History in the French Renaissance.*
       New York: Columbia University Press, 1970.
4:78   Michell, Alan. "German History in France After 1870," *Journal
       of Contemporary History,* vol. 2, no. 3 (1967), pp. 81-100.
4:79   Osburn, Charles B. *The Present State of French Studies.*
       Metuchen, N.J.: Scarecrow, 1971.
4:80   Rémond, René. "France: Work in Progress," *Journal of Con-
       temporary History,* vol. 2, no. 1 (1967), pp. 35-48.
4:81   Renouvin, Pierre. "Research in Modern and Contemporary
       History: Present Trends in France," *Journal of Modern History,*
       vol. 38, no. 1 (1966), pp. 1-12.
4:82   Rule, John C. "Paul Vaucher: Historian," *French Historical
       Studies,* vol. 5, no. 1 (1967), pp. 98-105.
4:83   Shapiro, Gilbert. "The Many Lives of Georges Lefebvre," *Ameri-
       can Historical Review,* vol. 72, no. 2 (1967), pp. 502-514.
4:84   ———, John Markoff and Sasha R. Weitman. "Quantitative
       Studies on the French Revolution," *History and Theory,* vol.
       12, no. 2 (1973), pp. 163-191.

GERMANY

4:85   Andrews, Herbert D. "Bismarck's Foreign Policy and German
       Historiography," *Journal of Modern History,* vol. 37, no. 3
       (1965), pp. 345-356.
4:86   Carsten, Francis L. "Arthur Rosenburg: Ancient Historian Into
       Leading Communist," *Journal of Contemporary History,* vol.
       8, no. 1 (1973), pp. 63-75.

4:87   Chamberlain, Houston Stewart. *Foundations of the Nineteenth
        Century.* Translated from German by John Lees. With an
        introduction by George L. Mosse. New York: H. Fertig, 1968.

4:88   Craig, Gordon. "Johannes von Müller: The Historian in Search
        of a Hero," *American Historical Review,* vol. 74, no. 5 (1969),
        pp. 1487-1502.

4:89   *Enlightenment Historiography: Three German Studies.* Middle-
        town, Conn.: Wesleyan University Press, 1971.

4:90   Gerhard, Dietrich. "Hajo Holborn: Reminiscences," *Central
        European History,* vol. 3, nos. 1-2 (1970), pp. 9-16.

4:91   ————. "Otto Hintze: His Work and Significance in Historiog-
        raphy," *Central European History,* vol. 3, nos. 1-2 (1970),
        pp. 17-48.

4:92   Harrison, Gordon Scott. "The Hanseatic League in Historical
        Interpretation," *Historian,* vol. 33, no. 3 (1971), pp. 385-397.

4:93   Herzfeld, Hans. "Germany: After the Catastrophe," *Journal of
        Contemporary History,* vol. 2, no. 1 (1967), pp. 79-91.

4:94   Iggers, Georg. "The Decline of the Classical National Tradition
        of German Historiography," *History and Theory,* vol. 6, no. 3
        (1967), pp. 382-412.

4:95   Kren, George M. "Political Implications of German Historicism,"
        Rocky Mountain Social Science Journal, vol. 6, no. 1 (1969),
        pp. 91-99.

4:96   Löwenstein-Wertheim-Freudenberg, Hubertus. *The Germans in
        History.* New York: AMS Press, 1969 [1945].

4:97   McClelland, Charles E. "Berlin Historians and German Politics,"
        Journal of Contemporary History, vol. 8, no. 3 (1973), pp.
        3-34.

4:98   ————. "History in the Service of Politics: A Reassessment of
        G. G. Gervinus," *Central European History,* vol. 4, no. 4
        (1971), pp. 371-388.

4:99   Moses, John A. "The Crisis in West German Historiography:
        Origins and Trends," *Historical Studies,* vol. 13, no. 52 (1969),
        pp. 445-459.

4:100   Sheehan, James L. "Germany 1890-1918: A Survey of Recent
        Research," *Central European History,* vol. 1, no. 4 (1968),
        pp. 345-372.

4:101   Werner, Karl Ferdinand. "On Some Examples of the National-

Socialist View of History," *Journal of Contemporary History*,
vol. 3, no. 2 (1968), pp. 193-206.

GREAT BRITAIN

4:102   Brentano, Robert. "The Sounds of Stubbs," *Journal of British
Studies*, vol. 6, no. 2 (1967), pp. 1-14.

4:103   Butterfield, H. "Some Trends in Scholarship 1868-1968, In the
Field of Modern History," *Transactions of the Royal Historical
Society*, vol. 19, series 5 (1969), pp. 159-184.

4:104   Chancellor, Valerie E. *History for Their Masters: Opinions in
the English History Textbooks: 1800-1914.* New York: A. M.
Kelley, 1970.

4:105   Connell, John. "Official History and the Unofficial Historian,"
Journal of the Royal United Service Institution, vol. 110, no.
640 (1965), pp. 329-334.

4:106   Elrington, C. R., ed. *Handbook for Editors and Authors of the
Victorian History of the Counties of England.* London: University of London, 1970.

4:107   Fell, Albert Prior, comp. *Histories and Historians: A Selection
of Articles From History Today.* Edited, with an original
introductory essay by Albert Prior Fell. Edinburgh and
London: Oliver & Boyd, 1968.

4:108   Green, John Richard. *Stray Studies, Second Series.* Freeport,
N.Y.: Books for Libraries Press, 1972 [1903].

4:109   Hale, John Rigby, ed. *The Evolution of British Historiography:
From Bacon to Namier.* London, Melbourne: Macmillan,
1967.

4:110   Hart, Jennifer. "Nineteenth Century Social Reform: A Tory
Interpretation of History," *Past and Present*, no. 31 (1965),
pp. 39-61.

4:111   Macray, William Dunn. *A Manual of British Historians to A.D.
1600. Containing a Chronological Account of the Early
Chroniclers and Monkish Writers, Their Printed Works and
Unpublished MSS.* Naarden: Anton W. van Bekhoven, 1967.

4:112   McCartney, Donal. "The Political Use of History in the Work
of Arthur Griffith," *Journal of Contemporary History*, vol. 8,
no. 1 (1973), pp. 3-19.

4:113   Marsh, Henry. *Dark Age Britain: Some Sources of History.* Hamden, Conn.: Archon Books, 1970.

4:114   Mathew, David. *Lord Acton and His Times.* University of Alabama Press, 1969.

4:115   Milne, Alexander Taylor. "The Victorian Historians," *Colorado Quarterly,* vol. 15, no. 4 (1967), pp. 301-317.

4:116   *Milton and Clarendon: Two Papers on 17th Century English Historiography Presented at a Seminar Held at the Clark Library on December 12, 1964.* By French R. Fogle and H. R. Trevor-Roper. Los Angeles: William Andrew Clark Memorial Library, University of California, 1965.

4:117   Mullins, Edward Lindsay Carson. *A Guide to the Historical and Archaeological Publications of Societies in England and Wales, 1901-1933.* Compiled for the Institute of Historical Research. London: Athlone Press, 1968.

4:118   Palais, Elliot S. "The Publications of the Royal Commission on Historical Manuscripts," *College and Research Libraries,* vol. 33, no. 2 (1972), pp. 113-118.

4:119   Ribner, Irving. *The English History Play in the Age of Shakespeare.* Revised edition. New York: Barnes & Noble, 1965.

4:120   Temperley, Howard. "American Studies in Britain," *American Quarterly,* vol. 18, no. 2, part 2 (1966), pp. 251-269.

4:121   Thomson, David. "The Writing of Contemporary History," *Journal of Contemporary History,* vol. 2, no. 1 (1967), pp. 25-34.

4:122   Williams, Eric Eustace. *British Historians and the West Indies.* Preface by Alan Bullock. New York: Scribner, 1967 [1964].

HUNGARY

4:123   Hanak, Peter. "Problems of East European History in Recent Hungarian Historiography," *East European Quarterly,* vol. 1, no. 2 (1967), pp. 123-142.

4:124   Varkonyi, A. R. "The Impact of Scientific Thinking on Hungarian Historiography About the Middle of the 19th Century," *Acta Historica,* vol. 14, no. 1-2 (1968), pp. 1-20.

INDIA

4:125 Ahmad, Aziz. "Approaches to History in the Late Nineteenth and Early Twentieth Century Muslim India," *Journal of World History*, vol. 9, no. 4 (1966), pp. 987-1008.

4:126 Ballhatchet, K. "Recent Historiography of the Raj," *Victorian Studies*, vol. 12, no. 4 (1969), pp. 458-461.

4:127 Broomfield, J. H. "The Regional Elites: A Theory of Modern Indian History," *Indian Economic and Social History Review*, vol. 3, no. 3 (1966), pp. 279-291.

4:128 Evans, Hubert. "Recent Soviet Writing on India," *Central Asian Review*, vol. 16, no. 2 (1968), pp. 110-121, 135; no. 3, pp. 229-243.

4:129 Fergusson, H. "Some Issues in South Asian History," *Quarterly Review of Historical Studies*, vol. 7, no. 1 (1967), pp. 23-28.

4:130 Luniya, Bhanwarlal Nathuram. *Some Historians of Medieval India.* Agra: Lakshmi Narain Agarwal, 1969.

4:131 Ranganathan, A. "Nehru – Historian and Man of Letters," *Indo-Asian Culture*, vol. 17, no. 1 (1968), pp. 39-56.

4:132 Ray, Sibnarayan. "India: After Independence," *Journal of Contemporary History*, vol. 2, no. 1 (1967), pp. 125-141.

4:133 Raychaudhuri, Tapan. "The Social Sciences and the Study of Indian Economic History," *International Social Science Journal*, vol. 17, no. 4 (1965), pp. 635-643.

ITALY

4:134 Bouwsma, William J. "Three Types of Historiography in Post-Renaissance Italy," *History and Theory*, vol. 4, no. 3 (1965), pp. 303-314.

4:135 Huppert, George. "The Renaissance Background of Historicism," *History and Theory*, vol. 5, no. 1 (1966), pp. 48-60.

4:136 Janik, Linda G. "Lorenzo Valla: The Primacy of Rhetoric and the Demoralization of History," *History and Theory*, vol. 12, no. 4 (1973), pp. 389-404.

4:137 Pavone, Claudio. "Italy: Trends and Problems," *Journal of Contemporary History*, vol. 2, no. 1 (1967), pp. 49-77.

4:138   Smith, Denis M. "Benedetto Croce: History and Politics,"
        Journal of Contemporary History, vol. 8, no. 1 (1973), pp.
        41-61.
4:139   Struever, Nancy S. *The Language of History in the Renaissance:
        Rhetoric and Historical Consciousness in Florentine Human-
        ism.* Princeton: Princeton University Press, 1970.
4:140   Vivarelli, Roberto. "Italy 1919-21: The Current State of
        Research," *Journal of Contemporary History,* vol. 3, no. 1
        (1968), pp. 103-112.
4:141   Wilcox, Donald J. *The Development of Florentine Humanist
        Historiography in the Fifteenth Century.* Cambridge, Mass.:
        Harvard University Press, 1969.

LABOR HISTORY

4:142   Berner, Richard C. "Labor History: Sources and Perspectives,"
        Pacific Northwest Quarterly, vol. 60, no. 1 (1969), pp. 31-33.
4:143   Drescher, Nuala McGann. "Three Problems for the Labor
        Historian," *Pacific Northwest Quarterly,* vol. 60, no. 1 (1969),
        pp. 29-31.
4:144   McNulty, Paul J. "Labor Problems and Labor Economics: The
        Roots of an Academic Discipline," *Labor History,* vol. 9, no. 2
        (1968), pp. 239-261.

LATIN AMERICA

4:145   Al'perovich, M. S. "Soviet Historiography of the Latin American
        Countries," *Latin American Research Review,* vol. 5, no. 1
        (1970), pp. 63-70.
4:146   Baughman, James P. "Recent Trends in the Business History of
        Latin America," *Business History,* vol. 39, no. 4 (1965), pp.
        425-438.
4:147   Blakemore, Harold. "The Chilean Revolution of 1891 and Its
        Historiography," *Hispanic American Historical Review,* vol.
        45, no. 2 (1965).
4:148   Blasier, Cole. "Studies of Social Revolution: Origins in Mexico,
        Bolivia and Cuba," *Latin American Research Review,* vol. 2,
        no. 3 (Summer 1967), pp. 28-64.

4:149   Bumgartner, Louis E. "The Shotgun Approach to Latin America," *South Atlantic Quarterly*, vol. 64, no. 2 (1965), pp. 188-193.

4:150   Campbell, Leon. "Historiography of the Peruvian Guerrilla Movement," *Latin American Research Review*, vol. 8, no. 1 (1973), pp. 44-70.

4:151   Cline, Howard, ed. *Latin American History: Essays on its Study and Teaching, 1898-1965.* 2 vols. Austin: Published for the Conference on Latin American History by the University of Texas Press, 1967.

4:152   Davis, Harold E. "The History of Ideas in Latin America," *Latin American Research Review*, vol. 3, no. 4 (Fall 1968), pp. 23-44.

4:153   ———. "Legal and Political Thought in Mexico," *Inter-American Law Review*, vol. 8, nos. 1-2 (1966), pp. 95-114.

4:154   ———. "Problems in the History of Ideas in Latin America," *Duquesne Review*, vol. 15, no. 2 (1970), pp. 243-253.

4:155   Dean, Warren. "Sources for the Study of Latin American Economic History: The Records of North American Private Enterprises," *Latin American Research Review*, vol. 3, no. 3 (Summer 1968), pp. 79-87.

4:156   Hale, Charles A. "The History of Ideas: Substantive and Methodological Aspects of the Thought of Leopoldo Zea," *Journal of Latin American Studies*, vol. 3, no. 1 (1971), pp. 59-70.

4:157   Hennessy, Alistair. "Artists, Intellectuals and Revolution: Recent Books on Mexico," *Journal of Latin American Studies*, vol. 3, no. 1 (1971), pp. 71-88.

5:158   Iglesia, Ramón. *Columbus, Cortés and Other Essays.* Translated and edited by Lesley B. Simpson. Berkeley: University of California Press, 1969.

4:159   Keen, Benjamin. "The Black Legend Revisited: Assumptions and Realities," *Hispanic American Historical Review*, vol. 49, no. 4 (1969), pp. 703-719.

4:160   Lockhart, James. "The Social History of Colonial Spanish America: Evolution and Potential," *Latin American Research Review*, vol. 7, no. 1 (1972), pp. 6-46.

4:161   McAlister, Lyle N. "Recent Research and Writings on the Role of the Military in Latin America," *Latin American Research Review*, vol. 2, no. 1 (1966), pp. 5-36.

4:162   McGreevey, William P. "Recent Research on the Economic
        History of Latin America," *Latin American Research Review*,
        vol. 3, no. 2 (Spring 1968), pp. 89-117.

4:163   Meyer, Michael and Robert Esquenazi-Mayo, eds. *Essays in
        Latin American Scholarship.* Lincoln: University of Nebraska
        Press, 1970.

4:164   ———. "Perspectives of Mexican Revolution Historiography,"
        New Mexico Historical Review, vol. 44, no. 2 (April 1969),
        pp. 167-180.

4:165   Mörner, Magnus. "The Spanish-American Hacienda: A Survey
        of Recent Literature and Debate," *Hispanic American Histori-
        cal Review*, vol. 53, no. 2 (1973), pp. 183-217.

4:166   Murra, John V. "Current Research and Prospects in Andean
        Ethnohistory," *Latin American Research Review*, vol. 5, no. 1
        (Spring 1970), pp. 3-36.

4:167   Oswald, J. Gregory. "Contemporary Soviet Research on Latin
        America," *Latin American Research Review*, vol. 1, no. 2
        (1966), pp. 77-96.

4:168   Palais, Eliot. "A Look at Publications on Latin American
        History and Social Sciences," *Latin American Digest*, vol. 7,
        no. 4 (1973), pp. 22-24.

4:169   Poppino, Rollie E. "Luis Gonzaga Jaeger, S.J., 1889-1963,"
        Hispanic American Historical Review, vol. 45, no. 1 (1865),
        pp. 99-100.

4:170   Richards, Edward B. "Marxism and Marxist Movements in Latin
        America in Recent Soviet Historical Writing," *Hispanic
        American Historical Review*, vol. 45, no. 4 (1965), pp. 577-590.

4:171   Robe, Stanley L. "Contemporary Trends in Folklore Research,"
        Latin American Research Review, vol. 2, no. 2 (Spring 1967),
        pp. 26-54.

4:172   Sable, Martin. *Latin American Urbanization: A Guide to the
        Literature, Organizations and Personnel.* Metuchen, N.J.:
        Scarecrow, 1971.

4:173   Smith, Peter H. "The Image of a Dictator: Gabriel García Moreno,"
        Hispanic American Historical Review, vol. 45, no. 1 (1965),
        pp. 1-24.

4:174   Spalding, Karen. "The Colonial Indian: Past and Future Research
        Perspectives," *Latin American Research Review*, vol. 7, no. 1
        (1972), pp. 47-76.

4:175   Steger, Hans-Albert, Achim Schrader and Jurgen Grabener. "Research on Latin America in the Federal Republic of Germany," *Latin American Research Review*, vol. 2, no. 3 (Summer 1967), pp. 99-118.

4:176   Suchlicki, Jaime. "Sources on Student Violence in Latin America: An Analysis of the Literature," *Latin American Research Review*, vol. 7, no. 3 (1972), pp. 31-48.

4:177   Toman, Susan F. "Don Salvador de Madariaga: A Provocative Interpreter of Spanish America," *South Atlantic Quarterly*, vol. 71, no. 2 (1972), pp. 257-267.

4:178   Torodash, Martin. "Colombus Historiography Since 1939," *Hispanic American Historical Review*, vol. 46, no. 4 (1966), pp. 409-425.

4:179   ————. "Magellan Historiography," *Hispanic American Historical Review*, vol. 51, no. 2 (1971), pp. 313-335.

4:180   Valdés, Nelson P. and Edwin Lieuwen, comps. *The Cuban Revolution, 1959-1969: A Research-Study Guide*. Albuquerque: University of New Mexico Press, 1971.

MEDICAL HISTORY

4:181   Ackerknecht, Erwin H. "A Plea for a 'Behaviorist' Approach in Writing the History of Medicine," *Journal of the History of Medicine and Allied Sciences*, vol. 22, no. 3 (1967), pp. 211-214.

4:182   Klein, Randolph S. "The History of Medicine in Tudor Times: An Historiographical Survey," *Historian*, vol. 33, no. 3 (1971), pp. 365-384.

4:183   Rosen, George. "People, Disease, and Emotion: Some Newer Problems for Research in Medical History," *Bulletin of the History of Medicine*, vol. 41, no. 1 (1967), pp. 5-23.

MIDDLE EAST

4:184   Gabrieli, Francesco. *Arab Historians of the Crusades*. Selected and translated from the Arabic sources. Translated from Italian by E. J. Costello. London: Routledge & Kegan Paul, 1969.

4:185   Margoliouth, David Samuel. *Lectures on Arabic Historians,*

Delivered Before the University of Calcutta, February 1929.
New York: B. Franklin, 1972 [1930].
4:186 Owen, Roger. "Studying Islamic History," *Journal of Inter-disciplinary History,* vol. 4, no. 2 (1973), pp. 287-298.
4:187 Rosenthae, Franz. *A History of Muslim Historiography.* 2d revised edition. Leiden: E. J. Brill, 1968.

MILITARY HISTORY
4:188 Conn, Stetson. "The Army's Historical Program," *Military Review,* vol. 46, no. 5 (1966), pp. 40-47.
4:189 Higham, Robin. "A Facet of Military Intellectualism: The Memoirs of British Generals of the Second World War," *Journal of the Royal United Service Institution,* vol. 114, no. 654 (1969), pp. 59-63.
4:190 James, Robert Rhodes. "Britain: Soldiers and Biographers," *Journal of Contemporary History,* vol. 3, no. 1 (1968), pp. 89-101.
4:191 ———. "Thoughts on Writing Military History," *Journal of the Royal United Service Institution,* vol. 111, no. 642 (1966), pp. 99-109.
4:192 O'Neill, Robert. "Soldiers and Historians: Trends in Military History in the Nineteenth and Twentieth Centuries," *Journal of the Royal Australian Historical Society,* vol. 56, no. 1 (1970), pp. 36-47.
4:193 Smith, Arthur L., Jr. "History Writing and World War II," *Revue Militaire Genéralé,* no. 9 (1968), pp. 434-438.
4:194 Stacey, C. P. "The Life and Hard Times of an Official Historian," *Canadian Historical Review,* vol. 51, no. 1 (1970), pp. 21-46.

NETHERLANDS
4:195 Dunk, H. W. van der. "Holland: The Shock of 1940," *Journal of Contemporary History,* vol. 2, no. 1 (1967), pp. 169-182.
4:196 Huizinga, Johan. *Dutch Civilisation in the Seventeenth Century, and Other Essays.* Selected by Pieter Geyl and F. W. N. Hugenholtz; translated from the Dutch by Arnold J. Pomerans. London: Collins, 1968.

PACIFIC AREA

4:197 Davidson, J. W. "Problems of Pacific History," *Journal of Pacific History*, vol. 1 (1966), pp. 5-21.

4:198 Dening, Gregory. "Ethnohistory in Polynesia: The Value of Ethnohistorical Evidence," *Journal of Pacific History*, vol. 1 (1966), pp. 23-42.

4:199 Latukefu, Sione. "Oral Traditions: An Appraisal of Their Value in Historical Research in Tonga," *Journal of Pacific History*, vol. 3 (1968), pp. 135-143.

4:200 Maude, H. E. "Searching for Sources," *Journal of Pacific History*, vol. 3 (1968), pp. 210-222.

POLAND

4:201 Bromke, Adam. "Polish Communism: The Historians Look Again," *East Europe*, vol. 16, no. 12 (1967), pp. 20-27.

4:202 Polonsky, Antony. "The History of Inter-War Poland Today," *Survey*, no. 74-75 (1970), pp. 143-159.

4:203 Ryszka, Franciszek. "Poland: Some Recent Revaluations," *Journal of Contemporary History*, vol. 2, no. 1 (1967), pp. 107-123.

4:204 Troscianko, Wiktor. "Polish Historians: A New Day?," *East Europe*, vol. 16, no. 8 (1967), pp. 10-15.

SCANDINAVIA

4:205 Barton, H. A. "Historians of Scandinavia in the English-Speaking World Since 1945," *Scandinavian Studies*, vol. 40, no. 4 (1968), pp. 273-293.

4:206 Falnes, Oscar Julius. *National Romanticism in Norway*. New York: AMS Press, 1968.

4:207 Wahlback, Krister. "Sweden: Secrecy and Neutrality," *Journal of Contemporary History*, vol. 2, no. 1 (1967), pp. 183-191.

SCIENCE AND TECHNOLOGY

4:208 Cannon, Walter F. "P.S. If I Find Out What the Truth Is, I'll Drop You a Line," *Smithsonian Journal of History*, vol. 2, no. 2 (1967), pp. 1-24.

4:209   Price, Derek J. de Sola. "Is Technology Historically Independent of Science? A Study in Statistical Historiography," *Technology and Culture,* vol. 6, no. 4 (1965), pp. 553-568.

SPAIN

4:210   Jackson, Gabriel. "The Historical Writing of Jaime Vicens Vives," *American Historical Review,* vol. 75, no. 3 (1970), pp. 808-815.

4:211   Romero-Maura, Joaquín. "Spain: Civil War and After," *Journal of Contemporary History,* vol. 2, no. 1 (1967), pp. 157-168.

UNITED STATES

4:212   Adair, Douglass. "The Federalist Papers," *William and Mary Quarterly,* vol. 22, no. 1 (1965), pp. 131-139.

4:213   Angus-Butterworth, Lionel Milner. *Ten Master Historians.* Freeport, N.Y.: Books for Libraries Press, 1969 [1961].

2:214   Auerbach, Jerold S. "New Deal, Old Deal, or Raw Deal: Some Thoughts on New Left Historiography," *Journal of Southern History,* vol. 35, no. 1 (1969), pp. 18-30.

4:215   Bass, Herbert J., ed. *The State of American History.* Chicago: Quadrangle Books, 1969.

4:216   Bassett, John Spencer. *The Middle Crop of American Historians.* Freeport, N.Y.: Books for Libraries Press, 1966.

4:217   Beckmann, Alan C. "Hidden Themes in the Frontier Thesis: An Application of Psychoanalysis to Historiography," *Comparative Studies in Society and History,* vol. 8, no. 3 (1966), pp. 361-382.

4:218   Bogue, Allan G. "United States: The 'New' Political History," *Journal of Contemporary History,* vol. 3, no. 1 (1968), pp. 5-27.

4:219   Bowden, Henry W. "Science and the Idea of Church History: An American Debate," *Church History,* vol. 36, no. 3 (1967), pp. 308-326.

4:220   Boyd, Julian P. "A Modest Proposal to Meet an Urgent Need," *American Historical Review,* vol. 70, no. 2 (1965), pp. 329-349.

4:221 Brogan, D. W. "The Quarrel Over Charles Austin Beard and the
       American Constitution," *Economic History Review,* vol. 18,
       no. 1 (1965), pp. 199-223.
4:222 Brooks, John. "A Clean Break with the Past," *American Heritage,*
       August 1970, vol. 21, no. 5, pp. 4-7.
4:223 Brown, Robert E. *Carl Becker on History and the American
       Revolution.* East Lansing, Mich.: Spartan Press, 1970.
4:224 Burke, Joseph C. "Max Farrand Revisited: A New Look at
       Southern Sectionalism and Slavery in the Federal Conven-
       tion," *Duquesne Review,* vol. 12, no. 1 (1967), pp. 1-21.
4:225 Burwick, Fred L. "The Göttingen Influence on George Bancroft's
       Idea of Humanity," *Jahrbuch für Amerikastudien,* vol. 11
       (1966), pp. 194-212.
4:226 Bushman, Richard L. "The Future of Mormon History,"
       Dialogue: A Journal of Mormon Thought, vol. 1, no. 3 (1966),
       pp. 23-26.
4:227 Callcott, George H. *History in the United States, 1800-1860.
       Its Practice and Purpose.* Baltimore: John Hopkins Press,
       1970.
4:228 Cappon, Lester J. "A Rationale for Historical Editing Past and
       Present," *William and Mary Quarterly,* vol. 23, no. 1 (1966),
       pp. 56-75.
4:229 Colbourn, H. Trevor. *The Lamp of Experience: Whig History
       and the Intellectual Origin of the American Revolution.*
       Chapel Hill, published for the Institute of Early American
       History and Culture at Williamsburg, Virginia, by the Uni-
       versity of North Carolina Press, 1965.
4:230 Commager, Henry Steele. "The Roots of Lawlessness," *Satur-
       day Review,* February 13, 1971, pp. 17-19, 63-64.
4:231 Crowe, Charles. "The Emergence of Progressive History,"
       Journal of the History of Ideas, vol. 27, no. 1 (1966), pp. 109-
       124.
4:232 Cunliffe, Marcus. *Pastmasters: Some Essays on American
       Historians.* Edited by Marcus Cunliffe and Robin W. Winks.
       1st ed. New York: Harper & Row, 1969.
4:233 ———. "What was the Matter with Henry Adams?," *Commen-
       tary,* vol. 39, no. 6 (1965), pp. 66-71.
4:234 Davis, Allen F. "The American Historians vs. The City," *Social*

Studies, vol. 56, no. 3 (1965), pp. 91-96; no. 4, pp. 127-135.

4:235 Desai, Meghnad. "Some Issues in Econometric History," *Economic History Review,* vol. 21, no. 1 (1968), pp. 1-16.

4:236 Donald, David. "The Grant Theme in American Historical Writing," *Journal of Historical Studies,* vol. 2, no. 3 (1969), pp. 186-201.

4:237 Evans, Howard V. "Current Trends in American and European Historiography," *Michigan Academician,* vol. 4, no. 2 (1971), pp. 143-160.

4:238 Fridley, Russel W. "The Uses of State and Local History," *History News,* vol. 23, no. 12 (1968), pp. 231-242.

4:239 Gay, Peter. *A Loss of Mastery: Puritan Historians in Colonial America.* Berkeley: University of California Press, 1966.

4:240 Gilpatrick, D. H. "Clio and the Columnists," *Proceedings of the South Carolina Historical Association* (1968), pp. 52-65.

4:241 Goldman, Martin S. "Black Arrival in American History: A Historiographical Look at the Sixties," *Social Studies,* vol. 62, no. 5 (1971), pp. 209-219.

4:242 Greene, Victor P. "Marcus Hansen as Historian," *Mid-Continent American Studies Journal,* vol. 8, no. 2 (1967), pp. 26-32.

4:243 Greenway, John. "The Austramerican West," *American West,* vol. 5, no. 1 (1968), pp. 33-37, 75-79.

4:244 Guggisberg, Hans. "The Uses of the European Past in American Historiography," *Journal of American History,* vol. 4, no. 1 (1970), pp. 1-18.

4:245 Hagan, William T. "On Writing the History of the American Indian," *Journal of Interdisciplinary History,* vol. 2, no. 1 (1971), pp. 149-154.

4:246 Hansen, Klaus J. "The Metamorphosis of the Kingdom of God: Toward a Reinterpretation of Mormon History," *Dialogue: A Journal of Mormon Thought,* vol. 1, no. 3 (1966), pp. 63-83.

4:247 Harrison, J. A. "Time and the American Historian," *South Atlantic Quarterly,* vol. 64, no. 3 (1965), pp. 362-366.

4:248 Hays, Samuel P. "The Social Analysis of American Political History, 1880-1920," *Political Science Quarterly,* vol. 80, no. 3 (1965), pp. 373-394.

4:249 Hexter, J. H. "Some American Observations," *Journal of*

Contemporary History, vol. 2, no. 1 (1967), pp. 5-23.

4:250   Higham, John, with Leonard Krieger and Felix Gilbert. *History.*
          Englewood Cliffs: Prentice-Hall, 1965.

4:251   ———. *Writing American History: Essays on Modern Scholar-*
          ship. Bloomington: Indiana University Press, 1970.

4:252   *Historiography and Urbanization: Essays in American History*
          in Honor of W. Stull Holt. Eric F. Goldman, ed. Port Wash-
          ington, N.Y.: Kennikat Press, 1968 [1941].

4:253   Hofstadter, Richard. "The Importance of Comity in American
          History," *The Columbia Forum,* vol. 13, no. 4, pp. 8-13.

4:254   ———. *The Progressive Historians: Turner, Beard, Parrington.*
          New York: Knopf, 1968.

4:255   Hoover, Dwight W. "The Diverging Paths of American Urban
          History," *American Quarterly,* vol. 20, no. 2, part 2 (1968),
          pp. 296-317.

4:256   ———. "From Clio With Love," *American Quarterly,* vol. 18,
          no. 1 (1966), pp. 104-108.

4:257   ———. "Some Comments on Recent United States Historiog-
          raphy," *American Quarterly,* vol. 17, no. 2, part 2 (1965),
          pp. 299-318.

4:258   Jacobs, Wilbur R. "Research in Agricultural History: Frederick
          Jackson Turner's View in 1922," *Agricultural History,* vol. 42,
          no. 1 (1968), pp. 15-22.

4:259   Jones, Houston Gwynne. *For History's Sake: The Preservation*
          and Publication of North Carolina History, 1663-1903.
          Chapel Hill: University of North Carolina Press, 1966.

4:260   Josephy, Alvin M., Jr. "Indians in History," *The Atlantic*
          Monthly, June 1970, vol. 225, no. 26, pp. 67-72.

4:261   Juricek, John T. "American Usage of the Word 'Frontier' from
          Colonial Times to Frederick Jackson Turner," *Proceedings*
          of the American Philosophical Society, vol. 110, no. 1 (1966),
          pp. 10-34.

4:262   Kernel, Stirling. "Pierson versus Turner: A Commentary on the
          Frontier Controversy," *Historical Studies,* vol. 14, no. 53
          (1969), pp. 3-18.

4:263   Kraditor, Aileen S. "American Radical Historians on Their
          Heritage," *Past and Present,* no. 56 (1972), pp. 136-153.

4:264   Krenkel, John H. "Bancroft's Assembly Line Histories,"

American History Illustrated, vol. 1, no. 10 (1967), pp. 44-49.

4:265   Kristol, Irving. "American Historians and the Democratic Idea," *American Scholar,* vol. 39, no. 1 (1970), pp. 89-104.

4:266   Lewis, Merrill. "Organic Metaphor and Edenic Myth in George Bancroft's History of the United States," *Journal of the History of Ideas,* vol. 26, no. 4 (1965), pp. 587-592.

4:267   Lieber, Todd M. "The Significance of the Frontier in the Writing of Antebellum Southern History," *Mississippi Quarterly,* vol. 22, no. 4 (1969), pp. 337-354.

4:268   Loewenheim, Francis L., ed. *The Historian and the Diplomat: The Role of History and Historians in American Foreign Policy.* With contributions by Herbert Feis and others. New York: Harper & Row, 1967.

4:269   Maddox, Robert F. "Four Eminent Historians: Amber, Callahan, Chitwood, Summers," *West Virginia History,* vol. 37, no. 4 (1966), pp. 296-308.

4:270   ————. "Wider Frontiers—Questions of War and Conflict in American History: The Strange Solution of Frederick Jackson Turner," *California Historical Society Quarterly,* vol. 37, no. 3 (1968), pp. 291-236.

4:271   Marshall, Lynn L., and Seymour Prescher. "American Historians and Tocqueville's Democracy," *Journal of American History,* vol. 55, no. 3 (1968), pp. 512-532.

4:272   Mason, Bernard. "The Heritage of Carl Becker: The Historiography of the American Revolution," *New York Historical Society Quarterly,* vol. 53, no. 2 (1969), pp. 127-147.

4:273   Mathews, Joseph J. "The Study of History in the South," *Journal of Southern History,* vol. 31, no. 1 (1965), pp. 3-20.

4:274   McCoy, Donald R. "Underdeveloped Sources of Understanding in American History," *Journal of American History,* vol. 54, no. 2 (1967), pp. 255-270.

4:275   Merrens, H. Roy. "Historical Geography and Early American History," *William and Mary Quarterly,* vol. 22, no. 4 (pp. 529-548).

4:276   Morton, Marian J. *The Terrors of Ideological Politics: Liberal Historians in a Conservative Mood.* Cleveland: Press of Case Western Reserve University, 1972.

4:277   Mowry, George E. "The Uses of History by Recent Presidents,"
        Journal of American History, vol. 53, no. 1 (1966), pp. 5-18.
4:278   Newby, I. A. "Historians and Negroes," *Journal of Negro
        History,* vol. 54, no. 1 (1969), pp. 32-47.
4:279   Newton, Craig A. "Louis Girardin's Republican View of the
        American Past," *Radford Review,* vol. 20, no. 1 (1966), pp.
        5-17.
4:280   O'Brian, Michael. "C. Van Woodward and the Burden of Southern
        Liberalism," *American Historical Review,* vol. 78, no. 3 (1973),
        pp. 589-604.
4:281   Odum, Howard Washington, ed. *American Masters of Social
        Science: An Approach to the Study of the Social Sciences
        Through a Neglected Field of Biography.* By Howard W. Odum
        and others. Port Washington, N.Y.: Kennikat Press, 1965
        [1927].
4:282   Parkman, Francis. *The Correspondence of Francis Parkman and
        Henry Stevens, 1845-1885.* John Buechler, ed. Philadelphia:
        American Philosophical Society, 1967.
4:283   Pearce, T. M., and Mabel Major. *Southwest Heritage: A Literary
        History with Bibliography.* Albuquerque: University of New
        Mexico Press, 1970.
4:284   Petras, James. "US-Latin American Studies: A Critical Reassess-
        ment," *Science and Society,* vol. 32, no. 2 (1968), pp. 148-
        168.
4:285   Pierce, Richard A. "New Light on Ivan Petroff, Historian of
        Alaska," *Pacific Northwest Quarterly,* vol. 59, no. 1 (1968),
        pp. 1-10.
4:286   Qualey, Carlton C. "Marcus Lee Hansen," *Mid-Continent
        American Studies Journal,* vol. 8, no. 2 (1967), pp. 18-25.
4:287   Rodgers, Hugh I. "Charles A. Beard, The 'New Physics' and
        Historical Relativity," *Historian,* vol. 30, no. 2 (1968), pp.
        545-560.
4:288   Rosenberg, John S. "Toward a New Civil War Revisionism,"
        American Scholar, vol. 38, no. 2 (1969), pp. 250-272.
4:289   Ruetten, Richard T. "Sources of Fiction in Recent American
        History," *Social Studies,* vol. 56, no. 7 (1965), pp. 254-
        263.
4:290   Scheiber, Harry N. "At the Borderland of Law and Economic

History: The Contributions of Willard Hurst," *American Historical Review,* vol. 75, no. 3 (1970), pp. 744-756.

4:291   Schilling, Hanna-Beate. "Cotton Mather's *Politics and Sainthood,*" *Jahrbuch für Amerikastudien,* vol. 11 (1966), pp. 251-255.

4:292   Shaffer, Arthur. "John Daly Burk's *History of Virginia* and the Development of American National History," *Virginia Magazine of History and Biography,* vol. 77, no. 3 (1969), pp. 336-346.

4:293   Shalhope, Robert E. "Toward a Republican Synthesis: The Emergence of an Understanding in American Historiography," *William and Mary Quarterly,* vol. 29, no. 1 (1972), pp. 38-48.

4:294   Shaw, Peter. "Blood Is Thicker than Irony: Henry Adams' *History,*" *New England Quarterly,* vol. 40, no. 2 (1967), pp. 163-187.

4:295   Skotheim, Robert Allen. *American Intellectual Histories and Historians.* Princeton, N.J.: Princeton University Press, 1966.

4:296   Soltow, James H. "Recent Development in United States History," *Annals of the American Academy of Political and Social Sciences,* vol. 375 (1968), pp. 176-195.

4:297   *Some Pathways in Twentieth-Century History: Essays in Honor of Reginald Charles McGrane.* Daniel R. Beaver, ed. Detroit: published for the University of Cincinnati by Wayne State University Press, 1969.

4:298   "The Spirit of '70," *Newsweek,* July 6, 1970, vol. 76, no. 1, pp. 18-34.

4:299   Starobin, Robert. "The Negro: A Central Theme in American History," *Journal of Contemporary History,* vol. 3, no. 2 (1968), pp. 37-53.

4:300   Thorpe, Earl E. *Black Historians.* New York: Morrow, 1971.

4:301   Tuttle, Frank W. "Some Unsettled Problems and Issues of Economic History," *Social Science,* vol. 42, no. 3 (1967), pp. 150-162.

4:302   Tuttle, William M., Jr. "Forerunners of Frederick Jackson Turner: Nineteenth-Century British Conservatives and the Frontier Thesis," *Agricultural History,* vol. 41, no. 3 (1967), pp. 219-227.

4:303   Unger, Irwin. "The New Left Versus the New History," *American Historical Review,* vol. 72, no. 4 (1967), pp. 1237-1263.

4:304   Voght, Martha. "Herbert Eugene Bolton as a Writer of Local
        History," *Southwestern Historical Quarterly*, vol. 72, no. 3
        (1969), pp. 313-323.
4:305   Wallace, Lillian Parker, and William C. Askew, eds. *Power,
        Public Opinion and Diplomacy: Essays in Honor of Eber
        Malcolm Carroll by His Former Students.* Contributors Lillian
        Parker Wallace and others. Freeport, N.Y.: Books for Libraries
        Press, 1968 [1959].
4:306   Wesley, Charles H. "W. E. B. DuBois–The Historian," *Journal
        of Negro History*, vol. 50, no. 3 (1965), pp. 147-162.
4:307   Williams, Burton J. "The Twentieth Century American West:
        The Old Versus the New," *Rocky Mountain Social Science
        Journal*, vol. 6, no. 2 (1969), pp. 162-167.
4:308   Wilson, R. Jackson. "United States: The Reassessment of
        Liberalism," *Journal of Contemporary History*, vol. 2, no. 1
        (1967), pp. 93-105.
4:309   Wilson, William H. "Two New Deals: A Valid Concept?,"
        Historian, vol. 28, no. 2 (1966), pp. 268-288.
4:310   Wish, Harvey. "The American Historian and the New Con-
        servatism," *South Atlantic Quarterly*, vol. 65, no. 2 (1966),
        pp. 178-191.
4:311   ———. "The New Formalism versus the Progressive Historians,"
        South Atlantic Quarterly, vol. 67, no. 1 (1968), pp. 78-93.
4:312   Woodward, C. Vann. "The Future of the Past," *American
        Historical Review*, vol. 75, no. 3 (1970), pp. 711-726.
4:313   Young, Mary. "The West and American Cultural Identity: Old
        Themes and New Variations," *Western Historical Quarterly*,
        vol. 1, no. 2 (1970), pp. 137-160.

U.S.S.R.

4:314   Alexander, John T. "Recent Soviet Historiography on the
        Pugachev Revolt," *Canadian Slavic Studies*, vol. 4, no. 3
        (1970), pp. 602-617.
4:315   Allen, Robert V. "Recent Developments in the History of the
        Soviet Union and Eastern Europe," *Annals of the American
        Academy of Political and Social Science*, vol. 365 (1966), pp.
        147-160.

4:316 Baron, Samuel H. "The Transition from Feudalism to Capitalism in Russia: A Major Soviet Historical Controversy," *American Historical Review,* vol. 77, no. 3 (1972), pp. 715-729.

4:317 Black, Cyril E. "Marxism and Modernization," *Slavic Review,* vol. 29, no. 2 (1970), pp. 182-186.

4:318 Bolkhovitinov, N. N. "The Study of United States History in the Soviet Union," *American Historical Review,* vol. 74, no. 4 (1969), pp. 1221-1242.

4:319 Enteen, George M. "Soviet Historians Review Their Own Past: The Rehabilitation of M. N. Pokrovsky," *Soviet Studies,* vol. 20, no. 3 (1969), pp. 306-320.

4:320 Fleron, F. J., Jr. "Soviet Area Studies and the Social Sciences: Some Methodological Problems in Communist Studies," *Soviet Studies,* vol. 19, no. 3 (1968), pp. 313-339.

4:321 Gati, Charles. "History, Social Science, and the Study of Soviet Foreign Policy," *Slavic Review,* vol. 29, no. 4 (1970), pp. 682-687.

4:322 Gefter, M. Ia., and V. L. Malkov. "Reply to a Questionnaire on Soviet Historiography," *History and Theory,* vol. 6, no. 2 (1967), pp. 180-207.

4:323 Horak, Stephan M. "Ukrainian Historiography, 1953-1963," *Slavic Review,* vol. 24, no. 2 (1965), pp. 258-272.

4:324 Lerner, Warren. "The Unperson in Communist Historiography," *South Atlantic Quarterly,* vol. 65, no. 4 (1966), pp. 438-447.

4:325 Marko, Kurt. "History and the Historians," *Survey,* no. 56 (1965), pp. 71-82.

4:326 Mazour, Anatole G. "V. O. Kliuchevsky: The Scholar and Teacher," *Russian Review,* vol. 32, no. 1 (1973), pp. 15-27.

4:327 ———. *The Writing of History in the Soviet Union.* Stanford: Hoover Institution, Stanford University Press, 1971.

4:328 Mendel, Arthur. "Current Soviet Theory of History: New Trends or Old?," *American Historical Review,* vol. 72, no. 1 (1966), pp. 50-73.

4:329 Orchard, George E. "The Historiography of Russian 'Feudalism,'" *Rocky Mountain Social Science Journal,* vol. 6, no. 2 (1969), pp. 66-71.

4:330 Oswald, J. Gregory. "The Development of Soviet Studies on Latin America," *Studies on the Soviet Union,* vol. 7, no. 3 (1968), pp. 70-83.

4:331   Putnam, George F. "Soviet Historians, Quantitative Methods
        and Digital Computers," *Computers and the Humanities*, vol.
        6, no. 1 (1971), pp. 23-30.
4:332   Roberts, Spencer E. *Soviet Historical Drama: Its Role in the
        Development of a National Mythology.* The Hague: M. Nijhoff,
        1965.
4:333   Rogger, Hans. "Politics, Ideology and History in the USSR: The
        Search for Coexistence," *Soviet Studies*, vol. 16, no. 3 (1965),
        pp. 253-275.
4:334   Solodovnikov, V. G. "African Studies in the USSR," *Journal of
        Modern African Studies*, vol. 4, no. 3 (1966), pp. 359-366.
4:335   Tillet, Lowell. *The Great Friendship: Soviet Historians on the
        Non-Russian Nationalities.* Chapel Hill: University of North
        Carolina Press, 1969.
4:336   Vol'skii, Victor V. "The Study of Latin America in the U.S.S.R.,"
        Latin American Research Review, vol. 3, no. 1 (Fall 1967),
        pp. 77-87.
4:337   Wheeler, Geoffrey. "Asian Studies in the Soviet Union," *Central
        Asian Review*, vol. 14, no. 3 (1966), pp. 232-240.

YUGOSLAVIA

4:338   Djordjevic, Dimitrije. "Contemporary Yugoslav Historiography,"
        East European Quarterly, vol. 1, no. 1 (1967), pp. 75-86.
4:339   ———. "Historians in Politics: Slobodan Javanovic," *Journal
        of Contemporary History*, vol. 8, no. 1 (1973), pp. 21-40.
4:340   Dorotich, D. "Yugoslav Historiography on Yugoslavia's Foreign
        Relations Between the Two World Wars," *Canadian Slavonic
        Papers*, vol. 10, no. 2 (1968), pp. 166-179.
4:341   Halpern, Joel M., and E. A. Hammel. "Observations on the Intel-
        lectual History of Ethnology and Other Social Sciences in
        Yugoslavia," *Comparative Studies in Society and History*,
        vol. 11, no. 1 (1969), pp. 17-26.

APPENDIX
SELECTED LIST OF PERIODICALS
FOR STUDY AND AS PUBLICATION OUTLETS

The historian who is interested in historiography, research methods, philosophy of history, or teaching methodology has hundreds of periodicals available to him either as sources of professional reading or as potential outlets for the publication of research articles. Listed below are but a few of the leading periodicals to which writers may submit manuscripts or query letters regarding projected articles. More detailed information on these and hundreds more periodicals may be found in Alexander S. Birkos and Lewis A. Tambs, *Academic Writer's Guide to Periodicals*, 2 vols., Kent, Ohio: The Kent State University Press, 1971- .

HISTORIOGRAPHY, RESEARCH METHODS, AND PHILOSOPHY OF HISTORY

Abraxas: A Journal for the Theoretical Study of Philosophy, the Humanities, and the Social Sciences. Jorge García-Gómez, editor. Humanities Division, Southampton College, Southampton, New York 11968. Quarterly, 1970- . Worldwide in scope and covers theoretical aspects of historiography and philosophy of history. Contains book reviews, bibliographies, critical notes and translations of non-English materials. Potential contributors must send a query letter before submitting a completed manuscript. Interested in articles of a theoretical nature that are 15 to 30 typewritten pages and which conform to the Chicago style manual.

African Notes. Bolanle Awe, editor. Institute of African Studies, University of Ibadan, Ibadan, Nigeria. Semiannual, 1963- . Publishes articles on a wide range of topics dealing with African studies, including material that is relevant to Latin America, the West Indies, and the United States. Has no restrictions on chronological periods that are covered. Wants article manuscripts of no more than 10,000 words that cover interdisciplinary matters, historiography, and new research methods.

Agora: Journal of Humanities and Social Science. Martin A. Bertman, editor. State University of New York, College at Potsdam, Potsdam, New York 13676. Semiannual, 1969- . Worldwide in geographical focus and no limitations on chronological periods. Book reviews. Authors are requested to send a query letter before submitting completed manuscripts. Prefers 15 to 20 typewritten pages. Manuscripts should conform to *PMLA* for style.

Al-Abhath: Quarterly Journal of the American University of Beirut. Mahmud Ali Ghul, editor. American University of Beirut, Beirut, Lebanon. Quarterly, 1948- . Devoted to the culture, history, historiography, and philosophy of history of the Arab-Islamic Middle East from 410 A.D. to the present. Articles appear in Arabic, English, French, or German. Book reviews. No query prior to submission of manuscripts required. Wants articles of 3,000 to 10,000 words in length.

American Archivist. Harold T. Pinkett, editor. National Archives, Washington, D.C. 20408. Quarterly, 1938- . Publishes articles on archives administration, records management, auxiliary historical disciplines, historiography, and research methods. Worldwide in scope. Also publishes archival news and notes section, and English-language abstracts of foreign articles. Potential authors are requested to send a query letter before submitting manuscripts, which should be between 15 and 20 typewritten pages and follow the *U.S. Government Printing Office Style Manual.*

American Historical Review. R. K. Webb, managing editor. 400 A Street S.E., Washington, D.C. 20003. Five times yearly, 1895- . Leading professional historical periodical in the United States, published by the American Historical Association. Covers all fields and periods of history. Book reviews and notices. Potential contributors should read the October 1970 issue, pp. 1577-1580 for editorial requirements before submitting manuscripts.

American Hungarian Review. Leslie Konnyu, editor. 5410 Kerth Road, St. Louis, Missouri 63128. Quarterly, 1963- . Publishes articles on art, literature, science, history, and historiography of Eastern Europe. No limitations on chronological periods that may be covered. Special interest in articles dealing with American-Hungarian relations. Book reviews. Potential contributors are requested to query before sending completed manuscripts. Articles should be about 4 to 5 typewritten pages in length with reference notes at end of manuscript. Also publishes books on American-Hungarian relations.

American Jewish Archives. Jacob R. Marcus and Stanley F. Chyet, editors. 3101 Clifton Avenue, Cincinnati, Ohio 45220. Semiannual, 1948- . Devoted to Jewish life and history of North and South America from 1492 to the present. Considers and occasionally publishes articles on auxiliary historical disciplines, historiography, and research methods. Book reviews. The April issue contains a list of recent library acquisitions of the Jewish Institute of Religion of Hebrew Union College. Authors are requested to query before submitting manuscripts.

American Jewish Historical Quarterly. Nathan M. Kaganoff, editor. 2 Thornton Road, Waltham, Massachusetts 02154. Quarterly, 1893- . Official organ of the American Jewish Historical Society. Publishes articles on a wide range of subjects (including auxiliary historical disciplines, historiography, philosophy of history, and research methods) on the history of the American Jewish community in North and South America, 1600 to present. Book reviews, bibliography section, professional news, and documents. A query letter is requested before the submission of completed articles, which should not be over 30 type-written pages. Wants articles that are scholarly and based on primary sources.

American Scholar. Hiram Haydn, editor. 1811 Q Street, N.W., Washington, D.C. 20009. Quarterly, 1932- . Published by Phi Beta Kappa. Covers all areas of the humanities and social sciences with no limitations on chronological periods. World wide in scope of interest. Book reviews. Occasionally publishes issues devoted to one theme or topic. Authors are requested to send a query letter first, addressed to the managing editor. Pays $150 for articles on acceptance.

American West. Donald E. Bower, editor. 599 College Avenue, Palo Alto, California 94306. Bimonthly, 1964- . Organ of the Western History Association. Publishes articles by professional and lay historians and writers on the history of the frontier and westward movement in the United States, Mexico, and Central America. Also interested in articles on the Historiography and philosophy of history of frontier areas. Authors should send a query letter first. Articles must be about 3,000-4,000 words in length. A style guidance sheet for authors is available on request. Pays $100-$300 for articles on acceptance.

The Americas: A Quarterly Review of Inter-American Cultural History. Francis F. Guest, editor. Box 34440, Washington, D.C. 20034. Quarterly, 1944- . Published by the Academy of American Franciscan History. Devoted to the history of North and South America with no

limitation on chronological periods that are covered. Publishes articles
on auxiliary historical disciplines, historiography, philosophy of history,
and research methods. Book reviews. No query letter necessary. Manuscripts should not be over 60 typewritten pages in length and must conform to the Chicago manual of style. Reference notes at end of text.
Authors receive $2 per printed page at the end of the year.

Amistad: Writings on Black History and Culture. Charles F. Harris,
editor. 201 East 50th Street, New York, New York 10022. Semiannual,
1969- . Publishes articles that are worldwide in scope on Black history
and culture. No limitations on chronological periods. Potential authors
should send a query letter before submitting their manuscripts. Articles
range from 5,000 to 10,000 words in length.

Annals of the American Academy of Political and Social Science.
Richard D. Lambert, editor. 3937 Chestnut Street, Philadelphia, Pennsylvania 19104. Bimonthly, 1890- . A leading periodical in the social sciences
and is worldwide in scope. Primarily limited to articles dealing with current affairs, but includes material on historiography, philosophy of
history, and research methods. Articles are of general survey types directed
at a general rather than a specialized reading audience. Book reviews and
special surveys on current research and state of art in various fields. Prospective authors must query first, does not accept unsolicited manuscripts

Arizona and the West. Harwood P. Hinton, editor. Library 308, University of Arizona, Tucson, Arizona 85721. Quarterly, 1959- . History
and historiography of the American Trans-Mississippi West. No limitations on chronological periods of coverage. Book reviews. Every issue
contains a brief dedication to an outstanding scholar specializing in the
history of the American West. Prospective authors should insure manuscripts conform to same style as *American Historical Review* and are
well documented.

Asian Affairs: Journal of the Royal Central Asian Society. Arthur
Russell, editor. 42 Devonshire Street, London W1N 1LN, England. Tri-
annual, 1901- . History and historiography of Central Asia from earliest
times to the present. Book reviews. Prospective authors should query
editor before submitting manuscripts.

Aztlan: Chicano Journal of the Social Sciences and the Arts. Deluvina
Hernandez, managing editor. Chicano Cultural Center, University of
California, 405 Hilgard Avenue, Los Angeles, California 90024. Semi-
annual, 1970- . Devoted to the social sciences relevant to Mexican-

American affairs. Book reviews. Manuscripts should not exceed 50 typewritten pages and must be accompanied with a one-page summary.

Balkan Studies. 4 Vas. Sophias, Thessaloniki, Greece. Semiannual,
1960- . Devoted to the culture, history, historiography, and philosophy
of history of Southeastern Europe. No restrictions on chronological
periods that are covered. Articles are published in English, French,
German, or Italian. Book reviews. Reports on conferences of interest to
Balkanologists. Query before submitting manuscripts.

Baltic Studies. Charles Schlacks, Jr., editor-in-chief. G7A Social
Sciences Building, University of Pittsburgh, Pittsburgh, Pennsylvania
15213. Two to four issues per year, 1972- . Articles on the civilization,
culture, and history of Estonia, Finland, Latvia, and Lithuania. Articles
published in English, French, German, or Russian. Book reviews. Authors
should send 3 copies of manuscript which should not be over 30 typed
pages.

Business History Review. James P. Baughman, editor. Baker Library
214-216 Soldiers Field, Boston, Massachusetts 02163. Quarterly, 1926- .
History, historiography, and methodology of business and economic
history of all areas and periods. Book reviews. Occasionally publishes an
issue devoted to one topic or area. Query before submitting completed
manuscripts.

Cashiers d'Études Africaines. 20 rue de la Baume, 75 Paris 8e, France.
Quarterly, 1960- . Covers all periods and aspects of African history, including auxiliary historical disciplines and historiography. Articles appear
in English or French. Book reviews and research reports. Query before
submitting completed manuscripts.

Canadian Journal of History. Ivo N. Lambi and J. M. Hayden, editors.
Box 384, Sub Post Office No. 6, Saskatoon, Saskatchewan, Canada.
Semiannual, 1966- . Covers all periods and aspects of world history, but
excludes history of Canada in its scope. Book reviews. Prospective
authors should insure their manuscripts conform to the MLA Style
Sheet and not exceed 35 typewritten pages.

Caribbean Quarterly. P.O. Box 42, Kingston 7, Jamaica, West Indies.
Quarterly, 1949- . Covers all periods of the cultural and social history,
development, and historiography of the West Indies. Book reviews.
Query before submitting manuscripts.

Caribbean Studies. Mrs. Sybil Lewis, editor. Institute of Caribbean
Studies, University of Puerto Rico, Rio Piedras, Puerto Rico 00931.

Quarterly, 1961- . Devoted to the culture, history, and historiography of
Mexico, Central America, and the West Indies from 1492 to the present.
Book reviews. Current bibliography of recent writings on the Caribbean
area. Authors should query first prior to submitting completed manuscripts.

   Catholic Historical Review. Rev. Robert Trisco, editor. 305 Mullen
Library, The Catholic University of America, Washington, D.C. 20017.
Quarterly, 1915- . Organ of the American Catholic Historical Association. Publishes articles on all periods and areas of the history, historiography, and philosophy of history of Roman Catholicism. Book reviews.
Professional news and reports on meetings. Wants articles that make use
of new source materials and offer a distinct contribution to historical
knowledge. Manuscripts must conform to the Chicago manual of style
and not exceed 30 typewritten pages.

   Centennial Review. David Mead, editor. 110 Morrill Hall, Michigan
State University, East Lansing, Michigan 48823. Quarterly, 1957- .
Publishes articles for college-educated general readers on a wide range
of disciplines, including historiography and philosophy of history. Manu-
scripts should follow MLA Style Sheet and not exceed 5,000 words.
Pays $25 on acceptance.

   Central European History. Douglas A. Unfug, editor. Emory University, Atlanta, Georgia 30322. Quarterly, 1968- . Devoted to studies
on the history and historiography of German-speaking Central Europe.
Covers all periods. Book reviews. Bibliographical surveys on recent
research. A "Suggestions and Debates" column points up new areas for
research. Wants manuscripts that conform to the MLA Style Sheet and
exhibit original scholarship. Also interested in comparative and interdisciplinary studies.

   Church History. Robert M. Grant, Martin E. Marty, and Jerald C.
Brauer, editors. Swift Hall, University of Chicago, Chicago, Illinois
60637. Quarterly, 1932- . Published by the American Society of
Church History. Covers all periods and areas of the history of Christianity, including auxiliary historical disciplines, historiography, and
philosophy of history. Book reviews. Bibliographical reviews. Abstracts
of dissertations. Authors should follow Chicago manual of style. Manuscripts are not to exceed 25 typewritten pages.

   Daedalus: Journal of the American Academy of Arts and Sciences.
Stephen R. Graubard, editor. 7 Linden Street, Cambridge, Massachusetts

02138. Publishes articles in the general area of the humanities. World-wide in scope. Authors must query first.

East European Quarterly. Stephen Fischer-Galati, editor. 216 Hellems Building, University of Colorado, Boulder, Colorado 80302. Quarterly, 1967- . Publishes articles on all periods of East European history, including auxiliary historical disciplines, historiography, and philosophy of history. Book reviews. Occasional issues on one theme. Authors should consult previous issues for style before submitting manuscripts.

European Studies Review. J. H. Shennan, editor. Department of History, University of Lancaster, Bailrigg, Lancaster, England. Quarterly, 1971- . Publishes articles on East and West European history in the period from the mid-15th century to 1945. Text is in English or French. Book reviews. Publishes critical English-language résumés of articles published in European languages. Manuscripts must conform to the Oxford University Press style manual and not exceed 8,000 words.

Hispanic American Historical Review. Stanley R. Ross, editor. Richardson Hall, University of Texas, Austin, Texas 78705. Quarterly, 1919- . Professional organ of the Conference on Latin American History. Covers all aspects and periods of the history of Latin America. Book reviews. Notes and Comments. Professional news. Authors should query first before submitting manuscripts.

The Historian: A Journal of History. William D. Metz, editor. Department of History, University of Rhode Island, Kingston, Rhode Island 02881. Quarterly, 1938- . Covers all periods and areas of world history. Manuscripts should conform to the Chicago manual of style, not exceed 6,000 words, and appeal to professional historians from many different fields.

Historical Journal. D. E. D. Beales, editor. Sidney Sussex College, Cambridge, England. Quarterly, 1923- . Covers world history, historiography, and philosophy of history relevant to the period from about 1400 to the present. Manuscripts should follow the style of Cambridge University Press and not exceed 8,000 words.

History. R. H. C. Davis, editor. School of History, University of Birmingham, P. O. Box 363, Birmingham 15, England. Quarterly, 1915- . Official organ of The Historical Association of the United Kingdom. Covers all aspects of world history. Manuscripts should conform to the style of Oxford University Press and not exceed 8,000 words. Book reviews. Occasional critical review articles of new textbooks.

110 SELECTED LIST OF PERIODICALS

History and Theory: Studies in the Philosophy of History. George H. Nadel, editor. Wesleyan Station, Middletown, Connecticut 06457. Tri-annual, 1960- . Devoted to the publication of studies dealing with auxiliary historical disciplines, historiography, philosophy of history, and research methods. Book reviews. Also publishes supplements which are collections of articles on a single theme. Prospective contributors should query editor for style guidance sheet.

History Today. Peter Quennell and Alan Hodge, editors. Bracken House, 10 Cannon Street, London E.C.4, England. Monthly, 1951- . All aspects and periods of world history. Book reviews. Also publishes notices of teaching vacancies. Query prior to submission of manuscript. Cash payment upon publication of article.

Horizon: Magazine of the Arts. Charles L. Mee, Jr., editor. 551 Fifth Avenue, New York, New York 10017. Quarterly, 1958- . Covers world history, historiography, history of ideas, and philosophy of history. Query prior to submission of manuscript. Demands high quality writing. Pays upon acceptance of article.

Inter-American Review of Bibliography. Armando Correia Pacheco, editor. Division of Philosophy and Letters, Pan American Union, Washington, D.C. 20006. Quarterly, 1951- . Publishes articles on the history of North and South America, including historiography and philosophy of history. Book reviews. Current bibliography section. Authors should query first as journal does not normally accept unsolicited articles. Pays up to $70 per article.

International Journal of Middle East Studies. Stanford J. Shaw, editor. Near Eastern Center, Ralph Bunche Hall, University of California, Los Angeles, California 90024. Quarterly, 1970- . All aspects of Middle Eastern history from 600 A.D. to current events. Articles appear in English, French, or German. Book reviews. Prospective contributors should study recent issues for guidance and policy regarding manuscripts.

International Social Science Journal. Peter Lengyel, editor. UNESCO, Place de Fontenoy, Paris 7e, France. Quarterly, 1948- . Covers all of the social sciences and publishes many articles on research methods. News items on specialized agencies of the United Nations, new periodicals, current programs of various institutes, employment opportunities, and news of forthcoming international conferences. Query first as each issue is topic oriented. Pays $100 upon acceptance.

Journal of African History. F. D. Fage, J. R. Gray, Sheila Marks, and

Roland Oliver, editors. School of Oriental and African Studies, University of London, London W.C.1, England. Quarterly, 1960- . Covers all periods and aspects of the history of Africa. Book reviews. Prospective contributors should study policy statement regarding manuscripts which is published in each issue.

Journal of American History. Martin Ridge, editor. Ballantine Hall, Indiana University, Bloomington, Indiana 47401. Quarterly, 1914- . Official organ of the Organization of American Historians. Articles focus on 19th and 20th century history of the United States. Book reviews. Professional news. Manuscripts should not exceed 9,000 words. Pays 1¼ cents per word upon publication of article.

Journal of Contemporary History. Walter Laqueur and George L. Mosse, editors. 4 Devonshire Street, London W1N 2BH, England. Quarterly, 1966- . Publishes articles on political, diplomatic, and social history of the world from 1914 to present. Also publishes studies on historiography and philosophy of history relating to the above period. No book reviews. Prospective authors may request a style guidance sheet for aid in preparing manuscripts.

Journal of Economic History. Robert E. Gallman, editor. Carroll Hall, University of North Carolina, Chapel Hill, North Carolina 27514. Quarterly, 1941- . Official journal of the Economic History Association. Covers all periods and aspects of economic history; worldwide in scope. Book reviews. Professional news. Authors will be sent a style guidance sheet upon request.

Journal of Inter-American Studies and World Affairs. Ione S. Wright, editor. P.O. Box 8134, University of Miami, Coral Gables, Florida 33124. Quarterly, 1958- . An interdisciplinary journal devoted to a wide range of topics relating to North and South America from the 19th century to the present. Articles appear in English, French, Portuguese, or Spanish. Book reviews. An information sheet is available on request for prospective contributors.

Journal of Interdisciplinary History. Robert I. Rotberg and Theodore K. Rabb, editors. Department of Political Science, M.I.T., Cambridge, Massachusetts 02139. Quarterly, 1970- . Publishes articles on the application of research methods of the behavioral and natural sciences to historical research. Articles appear in English, French, or German. Prospective authors must query first.

Journal of Modern History. William H. McNeill, editor. 1126 E.

59th Street, Chicago, Illinois 60637. Quarterly, 1929- . Devoted to historical and historiographical studies of Eastern and Western Europe, and Russia from the 16th century to 1950. Book reviews. A style guidance and editorial policy sheet is available to prospective authors upon request.

Journal of Near Eastern Studies. Robert D. Biggs, editor. 1155 E. 58th Street, Chicago, Illinois 60637. Quarterly, 1884- . Interested in historical studies of the Ancient Near East and of the Old Testament. Articles appear in English, French, or German. Book reviews. Query before submitting completed manuscripts.

Journal of Negro History. W. Augustus Low, editor. 1538 Ninth Street N.W., Washington, D.C. 20001. Quarterly, 1916- . Official publication of the Association for the Study of Negro Life and History. Covers all areas, periods, and aspects of Negro history, including historiography. Book reviews. Professional news. Query before submitting manuscripts.

Journal of Social History. Peter N. Stearns, editor. Box 3009, Rutgers University, New Brunswick, New Jersey 08903. Quarterly, 1967- . Worldwide coverage of social history throughout all periods. Book reviews. Manuscripts should conform to the Chicago manual of style and not exceed 30 typewritten pages.

Journal of the History of Ideas. Philip P. Wiener, editor. Temple University, Philadelphia, Pennsylvania 19122. Quarterly, 1940- . A leading periodical in the field of intellectual history, historiography, and philosophy of history. Worldwide in scope with no limitations on chronological periods covered. Book reviews. Prefers manuscripts of 12 to 30 typewritten pages in length.

Journal of the History of Medicine and Allied Sciences. Miss Elizabeth H. Thomson, editor. Historical Library, 333 Cedar Street, New Haven, Connecticut 06510. Quarterly, 1946- . Covers all areas and periods of the history of medicine and relevant auxiliary historical disciplines. Query before submitting manuscripts.

Journal of World History. Guy S. Metraux, editor. CLT/CS, UNESCO, Place de Fontenoy, Paris 7e, France. Quarterly, 1953- . All periods of world cultural history, including auxiliary historical disciplines, historiography, philosophy of history, and research methods. Book reviews. Articles appear in English, French, or Spanish. Prospective authors should query first. Cash payment negotiated.

Latin American Research Review. Thomas F. McGann, editor. Richardson Hall, University of Texas at Austin, Austin, Texas 78705. Triannual, 1965- . Organ of the Latin American Studies Association. Devoted primarily to research methods in Latin American Studies. Book reviews. Research in progress. Institutional research news. Query before submitting manuscripts.

Luso-Brazilian Review. Lloyd Kasten, editor. 1130 Van Hise Hall, University of Wisconsin, Madison, Wisconsin 53706. Semiannual, 1964- . History and historiography of Brazil and Portugal of all periods. Book reviews. Articles appear in English, French, German, Portuguese, or Spanish. Book reviews. Manuscripts should conform to the MLA Style Sheet and be a maximum of 30 typewritten pages.

Mankind: The Magazine of Popular History. Alvaro Cardona-Hine, 8060 Melrose Avenue, Los Angeles, California 90046. Monthly, 1966- . All aspects and periods of world history, including historiography and philosophy of history. Authors should query first. Pays $100-$500 upon acceptance. Articles must be written in an informative and entertaining style.

Military Affairs. Robin Higham, editor. Department of History, Kansas State University, Manhattan, Kansas 66506. Quarterly, 1937- . Official publication of the American Military Institute. Worldwide coverage of air, military, and naval history, including historiography, research methods, and philosophy and teaching of military history. Book reviews. Professional and archival news. Prospective authors should read the inside front cover for manuscript submission requirements.

Pacific Historical Review. Norris Hundley, editor. Ralph Bunche Hall, University of California, Los Angeles, California 90024. Quarterly, 1932- . Official publication of the Pacific Coast Branch of the American Historical Association. Devoted to the historical study of American expansionism to the Pacific Coast and postfrontier development of the American West, including studies on historiography, philosophy of history, and research methods. Book reviews. Professional news. Manuscripts should follow the Chicago style manual and not exceed 30 typewritten pages.

Past and Present. T. H. Aston, editor. Corpus Christi College, Oxford, England. Quarterly, 1952- . All periods and aspects of world history. Review essays. Prospective contributors should consult the editor regarding style requirements.

Rocky Mountain Social Science Journal. Sidney Heitman, editor. Social Science Building, Colorado State University, Fort Collins, Colorado 80521. Semiannual, 1963- . Published by the Rocky Mountain Social Science Association. General interdisciplinary articles in the social sciences, including historiography and research methods. Book reviews. Authors are requested to query before submitting manuscripts.

Russian Review. Dimitri von Mohrenschildt, editor. Hoover Institution, Stanford, California 94305. Quarterly, 1941- . Covers all periods and aspects of Russian and Soviet studies. Book reviews. Notes and documents. Query before submitting manuscripts.

Slavic Review: American Quarterly of Soviet and East European Studies. Donald W. Treadgold, editor. 503 Thomson Hall, University of Washington, Seattle, Washington 98105. Quarterly, 1941- . Official organ of the American Association for the Advancement of Slavic Studies. Covers all periods and aspects of East European and Russian history; interdisciplinary in scope. Book reviews. Professional news. Manuscripts should conform to the Chicago style manual and not exceed 25 typewritten pages.

Social Research. Arien Mack, editor. 66 West 12th Street, New York, New York 10011. Quarterly, 1934- . Interdisciplinary coverage of the social sciences, including historiography, philosophy of history, and research methods. Book reviews. Accepts manuscripts up to about 20 typewritten pages.

Social Science Quarterly. Charles M. Bonjean, editor. University of Texas at Austin, Austin, Texas 78712. Quarterly, 1920- . Official publication of the Southwestern Social Science Association. Worldwide in scope, covers all of the social sciences. Book reviews. Prospective contributors are urged to request the journal's style sheet before submitting manuscripts.

Speculum: A Journal of Mediaeval Studies. Paul Maevaert, editor. The Mediaeval Academy of America, 1430 Massachusetts Avenue, Cambridge, Massachusetts 02138. Quarterly, 1926- . Leading scholarly periodical in the field of mediaeval history. Frequently publishes articles on auxiliary historical disciplines, historiography, and philosophy of history. Book reviews. Bibliography of articles in American periodicals. Authors should follow the MLA Style Sheet in preparing manuscripts.

Studies in History and Society. T. C. R. Horn, editor. Department of History, Western Washington College, Bellingham, Washington 98225.

Semiannual, 1968- . All periods and areas of world history. Prospective authors should prepare manuscripts in conformance to the MLA Style Sheet.

Studies in the 20th Century. Stephen Goode, editor. P.O. Box 12, Troy, New York 12181. Semiannual, 1968- . World cultural and literary history, including auxiliary historical disciplines and historiography. Book reviews and review essays. Manuscripts should follow the MLA Style Sheet.

Terrae Incognitae: The Annals of the Society for the History of Discoveries. Bruce B. Solnick, editor. Department of History, State University of New York, Albany, New York 12203. Annual, 1969- . Scope is worldwide with relevance to studies on the history of discovery and exploration, including the historiography thereof. Prospective authors should query first.

Theory and Decision. The Editors, c/o Department of Economics, University of Saarland, Saarbruecken, West Germany. Quarterly, 1970- . Interdisciplinary and theoretical studies on the philosophy and method-ology of the social sciences. Book reviews. Style sheet available on request.

Twentieth Century. Michael Wynn Jones and Michael Ivens, editors. 3 Clements Inn, London WC2, England. Quarterly, 1877- . Publishes articles on a wide variety of subjects, including historiography, relative to the 20th century. Book reviews. Authors should query before sub-mitting manuscripts. Cash payment negotiated.

Virginia Quarterly Review: A National Journal of Literature and Discussion. Charlotte Kohler, editor. One West Range, Charlottesville, Virginia 22903. Quarterly, 1925- . Covers a broad, unrestricted range of subjects, including historiography and philosophy of history. Articles should not exceed 7,000 words. Pays $5 per published page.

Western Historical Quarterly. Leonard J. Arrington and S. George Ellsworth, editors. Utah State University, Logan, Utah 84321. Quarterly, 1970- . Official organ of the Western History Association. Devoted to studies on the history of the westward movement and frontier phenom-ena of Canada, Mexico, and the United States. Also interested in articles on historiography, philosophy of history, and research methods. Book reviews and biliographical listings. Manuscripts should conform to the Chicago style manual and not exceed 7,500 words.

Western Humanities Review. Jack Garlington, editor. 330 Spencer

Hall, University of Utah, Salt Lake City, Utah 84112. Quarterly, 1942- .
Publishes articles on the humanities which exhibit an interdisciplinary
approach to the subject matter, including auxiliary historical disciplines
and philosophy of history. No restrictions on chronological periods
covered. Book reviews. Prospective authors should follow the MLA
Style Sheet in preparing manuscripts and not exceed 3,500 words in
length.

William and Mary Quarterly. Lester J. Cappon, editor. P.O. Box
1298, Williamsburg, Virginia. Quarterly, 1892- . Published by the Institute of Early American History and Culture. Devoted exclusively to the
colonial period of American history and includes relevant articles on
historiography, philosophy of history, and research methods. Book
reviews and documents. Professional news. Prospective authors should
query first.

TEACHING OF HISTORY

Game Design. James F. Dunnigan and Albert A. Nofi, editors.
Simulations Publications, 34 East 23rd Street, New York, New York
10010. Bimonthly, 1971- . Articles on game design and simulations of
historical conflicts and events. Book reviews. Same publisher issues
Strategy and Tactics. Both periodicals contain material that can be used
in college courses.

History Teacher. Leon L. Bernard, editor. Room 61, Memorial Library,
Notre Dame, Indiana 46556. Quarterly, 1967- . Published by the History
Teachers' Association. Devoted to articles on history teaching at the col-
lege and secondary school levels. Manuscripts should conform to the
Chicago manual of style and not exceed 7,000 words.

The History Teacher. Frederic A. Youngs, Jr., editor. California State
University, Long Beach, California 90840. Quarterly, 1967- . Published
by the Society for History Education. Devoted to studies on world
history and the teaching of history at the university, community college,
or secondary school level. Book reviews. Reviews of recent media
materials. Articles should be about 6,000 to 8,000 words in length while
essays on new educational programs, curricula, or techniques should not
exceed 5,000 words.

New England Social Studies Bulletin. William O. Kellogg, editor.

St. Paul's School, Concord, New Hampshire 03301. Annual, 1897- . Published by the New England History Teachers Association. Publishes articles on history teaching techniques and programs at the secondary school level. Book reviews. Prospective contributors are requested to query before submitting manuscripts.

Social Education. Daniel Roselle, editor. National Council for the Social Studies, 1201 16th Street N.W., Washington, D.C. 20036. 8 times yearly, 1937- . Publishes articles on the teaching of the various social studies with some emphasis on the secondary school level. Book reviews. Discussion of new media materials. Interested in manuscripts of from 900 to 5,000 words in length and which show an innovative approach to teaching.

Social Science. Panos D. Bardis, editor. Toledo University, Toledo, Ohio 43606. Quarterly, 1924- . Covers all of the social sciences. Book reviews and research notes. Prospective authors should read recent issues for policy statement regarding manuscript submission.

Social Studies. Leonard B. Irwin, editor. McKinley Publishing Company, 112 S. New Broadway, Brooklawn, New Jersey 08030. 7 times yearly, 1909- . Publishes studies on social studies teaching, curriculum, and school administration. Manuscripts should be about 18 typewritten pages in length.

Teaching History. John Standen, editor. Gipsy Hill College, Kenry House, Kingston Hill, Surrey, England. Semiannual, 1969- . Published by the Historical Association of the United Kingdom. Publishes articles which stress a practical approach to the teaching of history. Book reviews. Query before submitting manuscripts.

World and the School: A Review for Teachers of Current International Affairs. Otto Pick and Julian Critchley, editors. 23/25 Abbey House, 8 Victoria Street, London SW 1, England. 3 times yearly, 1963- . Published by the Atlantic Information Centre for Teachers. Publishes articles on the teaching of the social studies and foreign affairs focusing on period of 1900 to the present. Each issue contains articles devoted to a single teaching topic. Authors should query before submitting manuscripts.

AUTHOR INDEX

Abbot, Wilbur Cortez 3:1
Abrams, Philip 1:1
Acheson, Dean Gooderham 3:2
Ackerknecht, Erwin H. 4:181
Acton, John Emerick Edward Dalberg
    Acton, Baron 3:3, 3:4, 3:5
Adair, Douglass 4:212
Adams, Brooks 3:6, 3:7
Adams, Herbert B. 2:A1
Adams, Richard 1:2, 1:3
Adorno, T. W. 3:8
Ahmad, Aziz 4:125
Albrektson, Bertil 3:9
Alexander, John T. 3:169, 4:314
Allen, Howard 1:33
Allen, Robert V. 2:B1, 4:315
Allen, Rodney F. 2:B122
Al'perovich, M. S. 4:145
Altic, Richard D. 1:4
Anderson, Eugene 4:61
Andrews, Herbert D. 4:85
Angus-Butterworth, Lionel Milner
    4:213
Anthony, Albert S. 2:B2
Apter, David E. 3:10
Arendt, Hannah 3:11
Arthur, C. J. 3:12
Ashley, Maurice 3:13
Askew, William C. 4:305
Atherton, John 3:14
Atkinson, Michael C. 2:B3
Auerbach, F. 2:B4
Auerbach, Jerold S. 4:214
Austin, Norman 4:10
Ausubel, Herman 3:15
Ayala, Francisco 3:16
Ayandele, E. A. 1:43, 4:1
Aydelotte, William O. 1:6

Bader, Thomas 2:A2
Bahr, Hans W. 3:17

Baird, Robert D. 1:7
Balik, Stanislav 4:49
Ballard, Martin 2:A3
Ballhatchet, K. 4:126
Balthasar, Hans Urs von 3:18, 3:19
Banner, Lois W. 3:20
Barcan, Alan 2:B5
Barlow, George 2:A4
Barnes, Henry E. 3:21, 3:22
Baron, Samuel H. 4:316
Barr, Robert D. 2:B6
Barraclough, Geoffrey 3:23
Bartley, Russell H. 4:38
Barton, H. A. 4:205
Bartosek, Karel 4:50
Barzun, Jacques 1:8, 1:9, 3:24
Bass, Herbert J. 4:215
Bassett, John Spencer 4:216
Baughman, James P. 4:42, 4:146
Beaumont, Roger A. 1:10
Beaver, Daniel 4:297
Becker, Carl Lotus 1:11, 3:25
Beckmann, Alan C. 4:217
Beer, E. S. de 1:12
Beidelman, T. O. 3:26
Bell, J. H. 3:27
Beloff, Max 3:28
Ben-Israel, Hedva 4:72
Bender, Richard O. 1:14
Bennett, Norman R. 1:60
Bennis, Warren G. 3:29
Benson, Lee 1:15
Bergier, Jean-Francois 4:53
Berkhof, Hendrikus 3:30
Berkhofer, Robert F. 1:16
Berkowitz, David Sandler 1:17
Berlin, Sir Isaiah 3:31
Bernstein, Barton J. 3:32
Berner, Richard C. 4:142
Besancon, Alain 1:18
Biddiss, Michael D. 3:33

119

Bietenholz, Peter G. 3:34
Billington, Monroe 2:A5
Birkos, A. S. 1:19, 1:20
Black, Cyril E. 4:317
Black, John Bennett 3:36
Blakemore, Harold 4:147
Blasier, Cole 4:148
Blassingame, John W. 2:A6
Block, Jack 1:21
Blondel, Maurice 3:37
Blows, Roger P. 2:A7
Blyth, Joan E. 2:B7, 2:B65
Boardman, Fon W., Jr. 3:38
Bodin, Jean 2:A8, 3:39
Bogue, Allan G. 1:43, 4:218
Bolingbroke, Henry Saint-John, 1st
    Viscount 3:40
Bolkhovitinov, N. N. 4:318
Boni, Felix 1:22
Borsodi, Ralph 3:41
Boulding, Kenneth 3:42
Bourke, Paul F. 3:43
Bowden, Henry W. 4:219
Bouwsma, William J. 4:134
Boyce, Arnold N. 2:B8
Boyd, Julian P. 4:220
Boyer, Calvin J. 1:23
Braaten, Carl E. 3:44
Bradley, Francis Herbert 3:45
Brandon, Samuel G. F. 3:46
Braudy, Leo 1:24
Braybrooke, David 3:47
Breck, Allen D. 3:35, 3:367
Brenner, Robert H. 3:48
Brentano, Robert 4:102
Bridenthal, Renate 4:11
Brogan, D. W. 4:221
Bromke, Adam 4:201
Brooke, Christopher N. L. 2:A9
Brooks, Geoffrey R. 2:B10
Brooks, George E. 4:2
Brooks, John 4:222
Brooks, Philip C. 1:26
Broomfield, J. H. 4:127
Brown, Godfrey 2:B11
Brown, Robert E. 4:223
Bruce, I. A. F. 4:12
Buah, F. 2:A10
Buckwald, Joel 2:B12
Buel, Richard, Jr. 3:49

Bumgartner, Louis E. 4:149
Burke, Colin B. 1:27
Burke, Joseph C. 4:224
Burke, Peter 4:59
Burnette, O. Lawrence, Jr. 1:28
Burns, E. Bradford 4:39
Burridge, K. O. L. 3:50
Burrow, John W. 3:51
Burston, W. H. 2:A11, 2:A37, 2:B63
Burwick, Fred L. 4:225
Bury, John B. 3:52
Bushman, Richard L. 4:226
Butler, David 1:29
Butterfield, Herbert 3:53, 3:54, 3:55,
    3:56, 4:103
Butterfield, L. H. 1:30
Buzanski, Peter M. 2:A12

Callcott, George 4:227
Campbell, Leon 4:150
Campa, Arthur L. 3:57
Canning, John 3:58
Cannon, Walter F. 4:208
Cantor, Norman F. 2:A13, 4:60
Cappon, Lester J. 4:228
Cardan, Paul 3:59
Careless, J. M. S. 4:45
Carlson, Don M. 2:B14
Carney, T. F. 1:31
Carpenter, Peter 2:A14
Carr, Herbert W. 3:60
Carsten, Francis L. 4:86
Cartwright, William H. 2:B15, 2:B16
Casserley, Julian Victor L. 3:61
Catchpole, Brian 2:B17
Cate, James Lea 2:A15, 4:61
Cavanaugh, Gerald 3:151
Chaadaev, Petr 3:63
Chadwick, Owen 3:64
Chamberlain, Houston Stewart 4:87
Chambers, Lenoir 3:65
Chancellor, Valerie E. 4:104
Chattopadhyaya, Debiprasad 3:67
Chesneaux, Jean 4:21
Chiffot, T. G. 3:68
Child, Sargent B. 1:32
Choundhry, L. P. 3:424
Clark, C. M. H. 3:69
Clegern, Wayne M. 2:A16
Cline, Howard 4:151

Clive, John   3:70
Clubb, Jerome M.   1:33
Cobb, John B.   3:400
Cobban, Alfred   4:73
Coblentz, Stanton A.   3:71
Cochrane, Charles N.   3:72
Cochrane, Thomas C.   3:73
Cohen, Hennig   1:34
Colacurcio, Michael   3:74
Colbourn, H.   4:229
Colby, Elbridge   3:75
Cole, Arthur H.   4:43
Cole, C. Robert   3:76
Cole, Donald B.   2:B18
Collingwood, Robin George   3:77
Collis, Maurice   3:78
Coltham, Jeanette B.   2:B19
Commager, Henry Steele   2:A19, 2:B20,
    2:B21, 3:79, 4:230
Conkin, Paul K.   3:80
Conly, Dale L.   2:B24
Conn, Stetson   4:188
Connell, John   4:105
Connolly, James M.   3:81
Conrad, Edna   2:B25
Conrad, Robert   4:40
Constantinescu, Miron   3:83
Cooke, Raymond M.   3:82
Cordier, Ralph W.   2:B26
Craig, Gordon   4:88
Crawford, R. M.   3:84
Creighton, Mandell, Bishop of London
    3:85
Croce, Benedetto   3:86, 3:87, 3:88
Cromer, Evelyn Baring   3:89
Cronin, Richard J.   3:90
Crookhall, Robert E.   2:B27
Crowe, Charles   4:231
Crozier, Dorothy   1:35
Cullman, Oscar   3:91
Cuneo, Ernest   3:92
Cunliffe, Marcus   4:231, 4:232
Curtin, Philip D.   1:36
Curtis, L. P., Jr.   1:37

Dabney, Virginius   3:65
Dance, E. H.   2:B28
Daniels, Robert V.   2:A20
Danto, Arthur C.   3:93
Davidson, J. W.   1:38, 1:39, 4:197

Davis, Allen F.   4:234
Davis, David B.   3:94
Davis, Gerald   2:A21
Davis, Harold E.   4:152, 4:153, 4:154
Davis, H. W. C.   3:121
Davis, Ralph H.   2:A22
Davisson, William I.   1:39, 1:40
Dawson, Christopher H.   3:95
Dean, Warren   4:155
Deluz-Chiva, Ariane   3:96
Den-Boer, W.   4:13
Dening, Gregory   4:198
DePillis, Mario S.   1:41
DeSai, Meghnad   4:235
Destler, Chester M.   3:97
Deva, Indra   3:98
Diãdichenko, V. A.   2:B29
Diesing, Paul   1:42
Dietl, Paul J.   3:99
Dilthey, Wilhelm   3:100
Dimond, Stanley E.   2:B30
Dixon, Elizabeth   1:110
Djordjecić, Dimitrije   4:338, 4:339
Docking, James W.   2:B31
Dollar, Charles M.   1:44, 1:45
Donagan, Alan   3:101
Donald, David   3:102, 3:103, 4:236
Donnitz, Myer   2:A22
Donovan, Timothy P.
D'Oronzio, Joseph C.
Dorotich, D.   4:340
Douch, Robert   2:B32
Dovring, Folke   3:104
Dowling, William C.   1:46
Downing, F. Gerald   3:105
Dozer, Donald M.   3:106
Draves, David D.   2:B33
Dray, William H.   1:47, 3:107, 3:108,
    3:109, 3:119
Drescher, Nuala McGann   4:143
Droysen, Johann Gustav   2:A24
Duberman, Martin   3:110, 3:111
Dunk, H. W. van der   4:195
Dunn, John   3:112
Dunner, Joseph   2:B34
Dunning, William A.   3:113
Durant, William James   3:114

Ebeling, Gerhard   3:115
Eckstein, Harry   3:116

Edwards, S. F. 2:A25
Eisenstein, Elizabeth 3:117
Ekman, Ernst 2:A26
Ellison, Ralph 3:118
Elrington, C. R. 4:106
Elton, Geoffrey R. 1:48, 1:49, 2:A27,
    2:A28, 2:A54
Ely, Richard 3:119
Emmet, Richard S. 2:A29
Engle, Shirley 2:B35
English, John C. 3:120
Enteen, George M. 2:A30, 4:319
Erickson, Edgar L. 2:B36
Esquenazi-Mayo, Roberto 4:163
Estrin, Jack C. 2:B37
Evans, Howard 4:237
Evans, Hubert 4:22, 4:23, 4:128

Fain, Haskell 3:124, 3:125
Fairley, John A. 2:B38
Faissler, Margareta 2:B39
Falnes, Oscar 4:206
Farmer, W. 3:126
Farrel, John K. 3:127
Febvre, Lucien P. V. 3:128
Feder, Bernard 2:B40
Feins, Daniel M. 2:B84
Feinstein, Howard 1:49, 1:50
Feis, Herbert 3:129
Feldmesser, Robert A. 2:B41
Fell, Albert Prior 3:130, 4:107
Fendelman, Earl B. 2:B42
Fenton, Edwin 2:B43
Ferguson, Sheila 2:B44
Fergusson, H. 4:129
Feuer, Lewis S. 3:13
Finberg, H. 1:51, 1:52
Fines, John 2:A31, 2:B19, 2:B45,
    2:B46, 2:B47
Finley, M. I. 4:14
Finnegan, Ruth 1:53
Firda, Richard A. 3:132
Fischer, David H. 1:54
Fisher, Herber A. L. 3:134
Fitzpatrick, Joseph L.
Fitzsimons, Matthew 3:135
Fitzsimons, Richard W.
Flechtheim, Ossip K. 3:136
Fleischer, Helmut 3:137

Fleming, John V. 1:55
Fleishman, Robert W. 3:138
Flender, Helmut 3:139
Fleron, F. J., Jr. 4:320
Flint, Robert 3:140
Floud, Roderick 1:56
Fogel, French R. 3:308, 4:116
Fogel, R. W. 1:43
Fornisano, Ronald P. 1:57
Fraenkel, Jack R. 2:B48
François, Michel 2:A44
Frédéricq, Paul 2:B49, 2:B50
Freeman, Edward Augustus 3:142
Frerichs, Allen H. 2:B51
Fridley, Russell W. 4:238
Fromm, Harold 3:143
Fuller, Daniel P. 1:58
Furet, Francois 3:144
Fyrth, Herbert, Jr. 1:59

Gabel, Creighton 1:60
Gabrieli, Francesco 4:24, 4:184
Galambos, Louis 1:61
Galbraith, John S. 3:145
Gall, Morris 2:B52
Gallis, W. B. 3:146
Gardiner, Patrick 3:147
Gati, Charles 4:321
Gautam, Brijendra Pratap 1:62
Gawronski, Donald V. 2:A32, 3:148
Gay, Peter 3:149, 3:150, 3:151,
    3:152, 4:239
Geddes, John A. 2:A33
Gefter, M. Ia. 4:322
Geismar, Peter 4:74
Gellner, Ernest 3:153
Gemorah, Solomon 1:63
Gentile, Giovanni 1:64
Gentles, Frederick 3:155
Georgeoff, John 2:B53
Gerhard, Dietrich 4:90, 4:91
Geyl, Pieter 3:156, 3:361
Gilb, Corinne Lathrop 3:157
Gilbert, Arthur N. 3:158
Gilbert, Felix 1:65, 1:66
Gillespie, Neal C. 3:159
Gilliom, Eugene M. 2:B54
Gilpatrick, D. H. 4:240
Glezerman, G. 3:160

Goddard, David 3:161
Goel, Dharmendra 3:162
Goldman, Eric F. 4:252
Goldman, Martin S. 4:241
Goldstein, Leon J. 3:163
Gooch, George P. 3:164, 3:165, 3:166
Good, John M. 2:B55
Goodman, Elizabeth J. 1:67
Gordon, David C. 4:3
Gore, John 3:167
Gosden, P. H. 2:B56
Gottschalk, Louis Reichenthal 1:68
Goubert, Pierre 4:75
Gould, J. B. 3:68
Graff, Henry F. 1:9
Graham, Gerald Sandford 3:169
Grannis, Joseph C. 2:A34
Grant, George P. 3:170
Grant, Michael 4:15
Gray, J. M. 3:171
Green, C. W. 2:A37, 2:B63
Green, John 4:108
Greene, Victor P. 4:242
Greenleaf, Richard E. 1:69
Greenway, John 4:243
Greever, Jeanet G. 2:B57
Griffiths, Naomi E. 2:B58
Grimes, Howard 3:172
Grivas, Theodore 2:A35
Grubber, Edward C. 2:A36
Gruner, Rolf 1:70, 3:119, 3:173
Grunfeld, Joseph 3:174
Guggisberg, Hans 4:244
Guilday, Peter 3:62
Gulick, Barbara 3:420
Gunnell, John G. 3:175

Hadkins, Lora 2:B60
Hagan, William T. 4:245
Hale, Charles 4:156
Hale, John R. 4:109
Hale, Richard W., Jr. 1:71
Hales, E. E. Y. 2:B61
Halle, Louis J. 3:176, 3:177
Halpern, Joel M. 4:341
Halperin, S. William 4:65
Halsey, Van R., Jr. 2:B62
Halvorson, John V. 3:178
Hammel, E. A. 4:341
Hampson, Norman 3:179

Hanak, Peter 4:123
Hancock, W. K. 1:72
Handlin, Oscar 3:180
Hanham, H. J. 1:73
Hanke, Lewis 2:A38
Hanks, Lucien M. 4:25
Hansen, Klaus J. 4:246
Hansen, Lorentz I. 2:A39
Hantula, James 2:B64
Happer, Eric 2:B65
Harder, Helmut C. 3:181
Hardwick, Francis C. 2:B66
Harper, Charles W., Jr. 2:A40
Harrison, Brian 2:A4, 2:A41
Harrison, Gordon S. 4:92
Harrison, J. A. 4:247
Hart, Jennifer 4:110
Hartwell, R. M. 1:74
Harvey, Van Austin 3:182
Hasslof, Olof 1:75
Hastie, Tom 2:B67
Haye, Kh. A. 3:183
Hayner, Paul Collins 3:184
Hays, Samuel P. 4:248
Healy, David F. 2:B68
Hearden, Harry 1:76
Hefner, Philip 3:185
Heilbronner, Robert 3:186
Hein, Steven A. 3:187
Heller, Louis G. 1:77
Hennessey, Alistair 4:157
Henry, L. 1:78
Hepworth, Philip 2:B69
Herbst, Jurgen 2:A42
Herder, Johann Gottfried von 3:188, 3:189, 3:190
Herlihy, David 4:44
Hermann, Charles F. 1:79
Herr, Richard 3:191
Herzfeld, Hans 4:93
Hexter, Jack H. 3:192, 3:193, 3:194, 3:195, 4:249
Higham, John 1:80, 3:196, 4:250, 4:251
Higham, Robin 4:189
Hinckley, Theodore C. 2:A43
Hobart, Michael 3:199
Hobsbawn, E. J. 3:200
Hodgson, Peter Crofts 3:201
Hodson, R. F. 1:5

Hoenstine, Floyd 1:81
Hoffman, Ross John Swartz 3:202
Hofstadter, Richard 1:93, 4:253,
  4:254
Hogeboom, Willard L. 2:B71, 3:203
Holborn, Hajo 3:204, 3:205
Hollinger, David A. 3:206, 3:207
Holm, Bernard 3:468
Holmes, Dorothy 1:32
Hooker, James R. 4:4
Hoover, Dwight W. 4:255, 4:256,
  4:257
Horak, Stephan M. 4:323
Horgan, Paul 3:208
Hornkheimer, Max 3:209
Hoyt, Nelly N. 3:210
Hudson, Charles 3:211
Hughes, H. Stuart 1:82, 3:212
Hughes, J. R. T. 4:54
Huizinga, Johan 4:196
Humboldt, Wilhelm von 3:213
Hunt, E. H. 4:55
Huppert, George 4:76, 4:135

Ibn, Khaldun 3:214
Iggers, Georg G. 3:215, 4:94
Iglesia, Ramón 4:158
Inglis, Kenneth S. 2:B73
Irwin, Leonard Bertram 2:B75

Jackson, Barbara (Ward) Lady 3:216
Jackson, Gabriel 3:217, 4:210
Jackson, Martin A. 1:84
Jacobs, Wilbur R. 1:85, 4:258
James, Bernard 3:218
James, Robert Rhodes 4:190, 4:191
Janik, Linda G. 4:136
Jansen, Mauris B. 4:26
Jarchow, Merrill W. 3:219
Jensen, Richard J. 1:45
Johnson, Allen 3:220
Johnson, William M. 3:221
Jones, D. H. 4:5
Jones, Gareth E. 2:A47
Jones, Grace 2:B77
Jones, Houston Gwynne 4:259
Jones, Howard Mumford 2:A48, 4:48
Jones, Thomas M. 2:A49
Jones, Tom Bard 1:86, 2:A50
Jones, W. R. 3:222, 3:223

Josephy, Alvin M., Jr. 4:260
Jouvenel, Bertrand de 3:224
Jovanovich, William 3:225
Juricek, John T. 4:261

Kahn, Shalom Jacob 3:226
Kármán, Mór 3:227
Kathleen, Sister M. 2:B78
Katz, Loren B. 2:B79
Katz, Michael B. 1:87
Katz, Solomon 4:16
Keen, Benjamin 4:159
Keir, Sir David 3:228
Keller, Charles R. 2:B80
Kelly, Donald R. 4:77
Kelly, Paul E. 2:B41
Kemnitz, Thomas M. 1:88
Keniston, Keith 3:229
Kennedy, D. E. 3:230
Kennedy, P. M. 3:231
Kent, George O. 3:232
Kent, Sherman 2:A51
Kernal, Stirling 4:262
Keyes, Gordon Lincoln 3:233
Kiefer, Howard 3:309
Kitagawa, Joseph M. 2:A52
Kitson-Clark, George S. R. 1:89,
  1:90, 2:A53, 2:A54
Klein, Randolph S. 4:182
Kochhar, S. K. 2:A55
Koenig, Duane 2:A56, 3:234
Kolakowski, Leszek 3:235
Konrad, Nikolai Isifovich 3:236
Kracauer, Siegfried 3:237, 3:238
Kraditor, Aileen S. 4:263
Kramnick, Isaac 3:239
Kren, George M. 4:95
Krenkel, John H. 4:264
Krieger, Leonard 3:240, 3:391
Kristol, Irving 4:265
Krout, John A. 3:241
Krug, Mark A. 3:242, 3:243
Kuehl, Warren F. 1:91
Kuhn, Thomas S. 3:244
Kuitert, Harmenus Martinus 3:245
Kuklick, Bruce 2:A57, 3:246
Kuzminski, Adrian 3:247

La Nauze, John Andrew 2:A58
Labriola, Antonio 3:249

Ladenburg, Thomas 2:B83
Landes, David 1:13, 2:A45, 2:A59
Lange, John 3:249
Langer, William L. 2:A60
Langlois, Charles Victor 2:A61
Langmuir, Gavin I. 3:250
Lapp, Paul W. 4:17
Laqueur, Walter 2:A46, 3:251, 3:387
Larkin, John A. 4:27
Latukefu, Sione 4:199
Laushey, David M. 2:A21
Lavnov, Petr L. 3:252
Lawler, Justus G. 3:253
Leff, Gordon 1:92, 3:254
Le Goff, Jacques 3:255
Lehmann, A. G. 3:256
Leinwald, Gerald 2:B84
Lerner, Warren 4:324
Levine, Norman 3:257
Lewis, Merrill 4:266
Lewry, Osmund 3:258
Lewy, Guenther 3:259
Lichtheim, George 3:260
Liddell-Hart, Basil H. 3:261
Liebel, Helen P. 3:262
Lieber, Todd M. 4:267
Lieuwen, Edwin 4:180
Lifton, Robert J. 3:263, 3:264, 3:265
Lindfors, Kenneth I. 2:B85
Lindsay, George 3:266
Ling, J. F. 3:267
Lipset, Seymour M. 1:93
Little, H. Ganse, Jr. 3:268, 3:269
Lloyd, E. R. 2:B86
Lockhart, James 4:160
Loewenheim, Francis L. 4:268
Logasa, Hannah 2:B87
Loper, William C. 3:270
Lord, Clifford L. 3:271
Lord, Donald C. 2:B88
Lorwin, Val R. 1:94, 1:95
Lottich, Kenneth V. 3:272
Louch, A. R. 3:273
Louis, William R. 3:274
Löwenstein-Wertheim-Freudenberg 4:96
Löwith, Karl 3:275, 3:276
Lowther, Lawrence 2:B89
Lucid, Robert F. 2:A62
Lukacs, John A. 3:277
Luniya, B. N. 4:130

Luthy, Herbert 3:278

MacIntosh, Henry Gordon 2:B90
Macray, William D. 4:111
McAlister, Lyle N. 4:161
McCall, Daniel F. 4:6
McCalmon, George 1:96
McCartney, Donal 4:112
McClelland, Charles E. 4:97, 4:98
McCoy, Donald R. 4:274
McCullagh, C. Behan 3:279, 3:280, 3:281
McGreevey, William P. 4:162
McMillan, N. 2:B91
McNatt, Norman 1:107
McNulty, Paul J. 4:144
Maddox, Robert F. 4:269, 4:270
Mahon, John K. 2:A63
Major, Mabel 4:283
Mallard, William 1:97
Mandelbaum, Maurice H. 1:98, 3:282, 3:283
Manuel, Frank E. 3:284, 3:285, 3:286
Marc-Wogau, Konrad 3:287
Marcus, John T. 3:288
Marczewski, Jean 1:99
Margoliouth, David S. 4:185
Marías, Julian 3:289
Marko, Kurt 4:325
Marks, Shula 4:7
Markus, Robert Austin 3:290
Marrou, Henri I. 3:291, 3:292
Marsak, Leonard M. 1:100
Marsh, Henry 4:113
Marshall, I. H. 3:293
Marshall, Lynn L. 4:271
Martin, Charles G. 3:294
Martin, Rex 3:295
Martorella, Peter H. 2:B92
Marvin, Francis S. 3:296
Marwick, Arthur 3:297
Marx, Karl 3:298
Mason, Bernard 4:272
Mathew, David 4:114
Mathews, Joseph J. 4:273
Maude, H. E. 4:200
Mays, David J. 3:65
Mazlish, Bruce 3:299, 3:300, 3:301, 3:302
Mazour, Anatole G. 4:326, 4:327

Mead, Sidney E.   3:303
Meel, Edward J.   2:A64
Meiburger, Anna   2:B93
Meiland, Jack W.   3:304, 3:305
Meinecke, Friedrich   3:306
Mendel, Arthur   4:328
Mendels, Franklin   4:66
Merrens, H. Roy   4:275
Meyer, Michael   1:69, 4:163, 4:164
Michell, Alan   4:78
Mieland, Jack W.   3:305, 3:306
Mikoletzky, H. L.   1:83
Milburn, Geoffrey   2:B94
Millar, T. B.   3:307
Millward, G. E.   4:18
Milne, Alexander Taylor   4:115
Mink, James   1:110
Mink, Louis O.   3:310, 3:311, 3:312
Mitchell, Roger   1:101
Moe, Christian   1:96
Mohan, Robert P.   3:313
Momigliano, Arnaldo   3:314, 3:315,
   3:316, 3:317, 4:19
Mommsen, Wolfgang   3:318
Montgomery, John W.   3:319
Moorsom, Norman   2:B96
Moraze, Charles   1:103
Morehead, Alan   3:320
Moreley, John Moreley   3:321
Morgan, Edmund Sears   2:B97
Morgan, George W.   3:322
Mörner, Magnus   2:A65, 4:165
Morton, Marian T.   4:276
Moses, John A.   4:99
Mosse, George L.   2:A46, 3:251, 3:387
Mowat, C. L.   2:B98
Mowry, George E.   4:277
Mozley, Ann   1:104
Mueller, M. G.   1:106
Mulhair, William   2:B115
Müller, Gert   3:323
Mullett, Charles F.   3:324
Mullins, Edward L. C.   4:117
Munitz, Milton E.   3:309
Munz, Peter   3:325
Murphey, Murray G.   3:326
Murphy, George G. S.   1:105, 1:106,
   3:327, 3:328, 3:329
Murra, John V.   4:166

Murray, Michael E.   3:320

Nadel, George   3:331
Namier, Sir Lewis Bernstein   3:323
Nappen, Marc   1:107
Nash, Ronald H.   3:333
Navone, John J.   3:334
Nevins, Allan   3:335
Nevinson, Henry Wood   3:336
Newby, I. A.   4:278
Newman, Fred D.   1:108
Newman, John Henry Cardinal   3:337
Newton, Craig A.   4:279
Neyland, Leedell W.   2:B99
Nichols, Roy Franklin   3:338
Niebuhr, Reinhold   3:340
Nield, Jonathan   2:B100
Nisbet, Robert A.   3:341, 3:342,
   3:343
Noggle, Burt   1:109
Norling, Bernard   3:344
Northeast, Peter   2:B101
Nota, Johannes Hille   3:345
Novack, George E.   3:346
Nowell, Charles E.   3:135
Nugent, Walter T. K.   2:A66

O'Brian, Michael   4:280
O'Brien, George   3:347
O'Malley, Joseph J.   3:351
O'Neill, Robert   4:192
Oakley, Francis   4:67
Ogden, H. V. S.   3:348
Odum, Howard W.   4:281
Ogelsby, John C. M.   4:46
Ogletree, Thomas W.   3:349
Olafson, Fredrick A.   3:350
Oman, Sir Charles William Chadwick
   3:352
Orchard, George E.   4:329
Ortega y Gasset, José   3:353
Osborne, Arthur   3:354
Osburn, Charles B.   4:79
Oswald, J. Gregory   4:167, 4:330
Outler, Albert C.   4:47
Owen, Rodger   4:186

Padden, R. C.   4:20
Paetow, Louis J.   4:63
Palais, Elliot   4:118, 4:168

Paluch, Stanley 3:355
Papaioannou, Kostas 3:356
Parker, Harold T. 3:191
Parkman, Francis 4:282
Parkinson, G. H. R. 3:357
Partin, Robert 3:358, 3:359
Patrides, C. A. 3:360
Patterson, Lloyd George 3:362
Pavone, Claudio 4:137
Pearce, T. M. 4:283
Pech, Stanley Z. 4:52
Peckham, Morse 3:363
Peiper, Josef 3:368
Pelikan, Jaroslav Jan 3:364
Penner, Hans H. 1:111
Perkins, Whitney 1:112
Perman, Dagmar Horna 2:A67
Peterson, Leland D. 3:366
Petras, James 4:284
Pflug, Gunther 1:113
Phillips, Derek L. 1:114
Pickens, William G. 2:B102
Pieper, Josef 3:368
Pierce, Donald John 3:369
Pierce, Richard A. 4:285
Pierre, Bessie Louise 2:A68
Pitt, David C. 1:115
Pius XI, Pope 3:370
Platt, Gerald M. 3:501
Plumb, J. H. 3:372, 3:373
Pocock, John 3:374
Pois, Robert A. 3:375
Pokora, Timoteus 3:376
Polanyi, Michael
Pollard, Sidney 3:377
Polonsky, Antony 4:202
Polos, Nicolas C. 3:378
Pompa, Leon 3:379
Pomper, Philip 1:116
Popper, Karl R. 3:380
Poppino, Rollie E. 4:169
Porter, Daniel R. 3:381
Post, John D. 3:382
Postan, M. M. 1:117, 3:383
Potdar, Datto Vaman 2:B103
Poulton, Helen T. 1:118
Prescher, Seymour 4:271
Pressly, Thomas 2:B18
Preston, Gillian 2:B104
Price, Derek J. de Sola 4:209

Price, Jacob M. 1:95, 1:119
Price, Joedd 2:A70
Price, Mary 2:B105
Pritzel, Konstantin 3:383
Pundeff, Marin V. 2:B106
Pundt, Alfred 3:135
Putnam, George F. 4:331

Qualey, Carlton C. 4:286

Rabb, Thomas 3:385
Rademeyer, J. L. 2:A86
Raghavachari, S. S. 3:386
Ranganathan, A. 4:131
Rashevsky, Nicolas 1:120
Rasila, Viljo 1:121
Ray, Sibnarayan 4:132
Raychaudhuri, Tapan 4:133
Redlich, Fritz 4:56
Reeves, Marjorie 3:388, 3:389
Regina, Mary 3:390
Reid, Inez Smith 2:A71
Rémond, René 4:80
Renouvin, Pierre 4:81
Rhodes, James Ford 3:393
Ribner, Irving 4:119
Richards, Edward B. 4:170
Richardson, Alan 3:394
Richardson, David B. 3:395
Richter, Melvin 3:396
Riesterer, Berthold P. 3:397
Roads, Christopher H. 3:398
Robe, Stanley L. 4:171
Roberts, Spencer E. 4:332
Robinson, James Harvey 3:399
Robinson, James McConkey 3:400
Rockwood, Raymond Oxley 3:401
Rodgers, Hugh I. 4:287
Rodine, Floyd 2:B89
Rogger, Hans 4:333
Rojas, Billy 2:B107
Roller, Duane 3:402
Romero-Maura, Joaquin 4:211
Romulo, Carlos P. 3:403
Roots, David E. 2:B108
Rosen, George 4:183
Rosen, Lawrence 3:404
Rosen, Philip 2:B109
Rosenberg, John S. 4:288
Rosenfield, Elizabeth S. 2:B121

Rosenthal, Franz 4:187
Rotenstreich, Nathan 3:405, 3:406
Rothblatt, Ben 3:66
Rothman, David 1:1, 1:79
Rothman, Stanley 3:407
Roucek, Joseph 2:A84
Rowney, Don Karl 1:122
Rubinoff, Lionel 3:408
Ruetten, Richard 4:289
Rule, John C. 4:82
Rundell, Walter, Jr. 1:123, 2:A72,
    2:A73, 2:A74, 2:B110, 2:B111
Runes, Dagobert 1:124
Rutman, Darret B. 3:409
Ryding, Nils Erik 1:125
Ryszka, Francizek 4:203

Sable, Martin 4:172
Sachs, Stephen M. 2:B112
Sakmann, Paul 1:126
Salvemini, Gaetano 3:410
Sanders, Jennings Bryan 3:411
Savelle, Max 3:412
Scheiber, Harry N. 4:290
Schellenberg, T. R. 1:127
Schilling, Hanna-Beate 4:291
Schlegel, Friedrich 3:413
Schlesinger, Arthur J. 3:414
Schlesinger, Arthur M., Jr. 3:415,
    3:416
Schmitt, Bernadotte Everly 3:417,
    4:68
Schmitt, Hans 4:69
Schneider, Richard L. 2:A13
Schofield, R. D. 1:128
Schouler, James 3:418
Schu, Pierre 3:419
Schuddekopf, Otto Ernst 2:B114
Schwartz, Stuart B. 4:41
Schweitzer, Arthur 4:57
Scudder, John R. 3:420
Seaberg, Stanley 2:B115
Seé, Henri Eugene 3:421
Selingsow, Mitchell 1:22
Sellen, Robert W. 2:B116
Sewell, William 3:422
Shafer, Boyd C. 2:A44
Shafer, Robert 1:129
Shaffer, Arthur 4:292
Shalhope, Robert E. 4:293

Shankel, George E. 3:423
Shapiro, Gilbert 4:83, 4:84
Sharma, B. M. 3:424
Sharrock, Roger 3:425
Shaw, Peter 4:294
Sheehan, James J. 4:100
Shera, Jesse Jauk 2:A76
Shiner, Larry 3:426
Shropshire, Olive E. 2:B117
Silby, Joel H. 1:130
Simon, H. Paul 3:427
Simon, Julian L. 1:131
Simmons, Charles E. P. 2:B57
Simms, L. Moody, Jr. 2:A77
Sinclair, Keith 3:428
Shivashankar, N. 3:429
Skinner, Andrew 3:430
Skinner, Quentin 3:431, 3:432
Skipp, V. H. T. 1:52
Skolnick, M. H. 1:132
Skotheim, Robert A. 3:433, 4:295
Small, Melvin 1:13
Smelser, Marshall 1:40
Smith, Arthur L., Jr. 4:193
Smith, Denis M. 4:138
Smith, Goldwin 2:A78, 3:434
Smith, John E. 3:435
Smith, Morton 1:134
Smith, Peter H. 4:173
Smith, Ronald G. 3:436
Solodovnikov, V. G. 4:334
Soltow, James H. 4:296
Somervell, David C. 3:437
Sorokin, Pitirim 3:361
Spalding, Karen 4:174
Spector, Robert M. 2:A79, 2:A80,
    2:B118
Spencer, Thomas E. 2:A81
Spitzer, Alan B. 3:438
Sprinzak, Ehud 3:439
Stacey, C. P. 4:194
Stalnaker, Robert 3:440
Starn, Randolph 3:441
Starobin, Robert 4:299
Starr, Chester 3:442
Stavrianos, L. S. 2:B119
Stearns, Peter N. 3:443
Steger, Hans-Albert 4:175
Stegner, Wallace 3:445
Steinfeld, Melvin 3:155

Steinkamp, John R.   2:B120
Stern, Fritz R.   3:391, 3:444
Steuwer, Rodger H.   3:446
Stevenson, W. Taylor   3:181, 3:447
Still, Bayrd   2:A82
Stinnette, Charles R.   3:448
Stocking, George W.   3:449
Stover, Robert C.   3:450, 3:451
Strong, Douglas H.   2:B121
Strong, Tracy B.   3:452
Strout, Cushing   3:453, 3:454
Struever, Nancy S.   4:139
Stubbs, William   4:70
Sturley, D. M.   3:455
Sturtevant, William C.   3:456
Suchlicki, Jaime   4:176
Sullivan, John E.   3:457
Sutherland, J. W.   2:A43
Sutherland, Lucy S.   3:458
Sweet, Paul R.   3:459, 4:37
Swift, Donald C.   2:B122
Symmons-Symonolewicz, Konstantin
    1:136
Szasz, Ferenc   3:460
Szreter, R.   1:137

Taft, William Howard   1:138
Tambs, Lewis A.   1:119, 1:120
Tapp, E. J.   3:461
Tarlton, Charles D.   3:462
Taylor, Alan John Percivale   3:463
Taylor, Donald S.   3:464
Taylor, Edmond   3:465
Taylor, Henry Osborn   3:466
Temperley, Howard   4:120
Thernstrom, Stephan   3:467
Tholfsen, Trygve   1:139
Thompson, James Westfall   2:A85,
    3:468
Thomson, David   2:A11, 3:469, 3:470
Thorne, Christopher G.   3:471
Thornton, Richard C.   4:29
Thorpe, Earl E.   4:300
Thruppe, Sylvia L.   1:140
Tignor, Robert L.   4:8
Tillet, Lowell   4:335
Tillinghast, Pardon E.   3:472
Tillot, P. M.   1:141
Tilly, Charles   1:13, 1:142, 1:143, 2:A45
Tocqueville, Alexis de   3:473

Todd, William   3:474
Toman, Susan   4:177
Topolski, Jerzy   1:144, 3:475
Torodash, Martin   4:178, 4:179
Toulmin, Stephen   3:476
Toynbee, Arnold Joseph   3:361,
    3:477, 3:478
Tresize, Robert L.   2:B123
Trevelyan, George Macaulay   3:479
Trevor-Roper, Hugh   3:308, 3:480,
    3:481, 4:71, 4:116
Troscianko, Wiktor   4:204
Trotter, F.   3:482
Trueman, John Herbert   2:B124,
    3:483
Tucker, K. A.   1:145
Turner, C. M.   1:146
Tuttle, Frank   4:301
Tuttle, Howard Nelson   3:484,
    4:302
Tuttle, William M., Jr

Unger, Irwin   3:485, 4:303

Vajreswari, R.   2:B125
Valdés, Nelson P.   4:180
Van Dyke, Mary   2:B25
Van Jaarsveld, Floris Albertus   2:A86
Vann, Richard T.   1:147
Vansina, Jan   1:148
Varkonyi, A. R.   4:124
Villari, Pasquale   3:487
Vincent, John Martin   1:149
Viner, Jacob   3:488
Vitzthum, Richard C.   1:150
Vivarelli, Roberto   4:140
Voght, Martha   4:304
Vol'skii, Victor M.   4:336
Voltaire, François Marie Arouet de
    3:489
Von Balthasar, Hans Urs   3:18, 3:19
Von Humboldt, Wilhelm   3:213
Von Laue, T. H.   3:490
Von Mises, Ludwig   3:49
Von Ranke, Leopold   3:492
Von Schlegel, Friedrich   3:413
Von Schiller, Friedrich   3:493
Vries, Leonard de   1:151

Wahlback, Krister   4:207

Wake, R. 2:B126
Wallace, Lillian P. 4:305
Walsh, William Henry 3:494
Wand, John W. C. 3:495
Wang, Gungwu 3:496, 4:30
Wansborough, John 4:9
Ward, Paul L. 2:A87
Ward, Russel Braddock Ware 3:497
Ware, Caroline 1:152
Warren, Donald, R. 2:A88
Warriner, Helen 2:A89
Washington, E. S. 2:B127
Wasiolek, Edward 3:498
Watson, Robert I. 1:153
Watt, Donald C. 3:499, 4:62
Watts, David G. 2:B128
Webb, Hershel 4:31
Webster, John C. B. 2:A75
Weideger, Stephen N. 2:B42
Weingartner, Rudolph 3:500
Weinstein, Fred 3:501
Weintraub, Karl Joachim 3:502
Wendel, Thomas 2:B129
Wenden, D. J. 2:A90
Werner, Karl Ferdinand 4:101
Wesley, Charles H. 4:306
Westcott, Roger W. 3:503
Whalley, Peter 3:504
Wheeler, Geoffrey 4:32, 4:337
White, Andrew 2:B130
White, Gerald T. 1:154
White, Hayden V. 3:486, 3:505, 3:506, 3:507
White, Morton Gabriel 3:508
White, T. M. 2:B130
Whitehill, Walter Muir 1:155
Widgery, Alban Gregory 3:509
Wilburn, Ralph G. 3:510
Wilcox, Donald J. 4:141

Wilde, Oscar 3:511
Wilkins, Burleigh 3:512
Williams, Burton H. 4:307
Williams, Eric Eustace 4:122
Wilson, Edmund 3:513
Wilson, Norman H. 2:B132
Wilson, R. Jackson 4:308
Wilson, William H. 4:309
Winkler, Fred H. 3:514
Winkler, Henry R. 2:A91
Winks, Robin W. 1:156, 4:232
Winters, Stanley B. 4:51
Wish, Harvey 4:310, 4:311
Witschi-Bernz, Astrid 3:515
Wittfogel, Karl A. 4:33
Wittke, Carl 3:122
Wolfson, Harry A. 3:516
Wolman, Benjamin 3:517
Woodbridge, Frederick J. E. 3:518
Woodruff, Douglas 3:141
Woodward, C. Vann 2:A92, 3:519, 3:520, 4:312
Woodward, Ralph L. 2:A93
Wright, Arthur F. 4:34
Wright, Monte D. 1:157
Wrobleski, Sergius 3:521
Wurgait, Lewis D. 3:522
Wylie, Kenneth C. 3:523

Yi Hong-jik 4:35
Young, J. D. 4:36
Young, Louise 3:524
Young, Mary 4:313
Young, Norman James 3:525
Young, Pauline 1:158
Yourgrau, Wolfgang 3:35, 3:367

Zinn, Howard 3:526